An Old Wife's Tale

An Old Wife's Tale

My Seven Decades in Love and War

Midge Decter

ReganBooks

An Imprint of HarperCollins*Publishers*

HarperCollins books may be purchased for educational, business, or sales
promotional use. For information please write: Special Markets Department, HarperCollins Publishers Inc., 10 East 53rd Street, New York,
NY 10022.

FIRST EDITION

Designed by Sarah Gubkin

Printed on acid-free paper

Library of Congress Cataloging-in-Publication Data

Decter, Midge.
    An old wife's tale : my seven decades in love and war / Midge
Decter.—1st ed.
        p. cm.
    ISBN 0-06-039428-5
    1. Decter, Midge. 2. Wives—United States—Biography. 3. Women—
United States—History. I. Title.
HQ1413.D28 A3 2001
305.4'092—dc21   2001019432

01 02 03 04 05 BVG/RRD 10 9 8 7 6 5 4 3 2 1

To the one but for whom

ACKNOWLEDGMENTS

I am grateful to my agent, Lynne Chu, for her immediate and cheering embrace of this book; to Judith Regan, my publisher, for hers; to Cassie Jones, my editor, for her tender attentions to my manuscript; to my daughters, Rachel Abrams, Naomi Munson, and Ruth Blum, for being so willing to let me into their lives and by doing so, teaching me so much; and above all, to my son, John, first reader, for his quick and loving eye.

CONTENTS

❧ Preface ❧

THE PAGES THAT FOLLOW offer a memoir of my life as a woman. Readers may be disappointed to discover that they contain no soul-searing confessions or tales of sexy adventure that nowadays seem almost to be obligatory. On the contrary, I am offering these ruminations on my life out of the belief that, save for the individual details, what has happened to me over the course of the past seven decades has in one way or another happened to many if not all present-day American women— from the almost dizzyingly rapid ringing of changes to the discovery of that in our lives which is never-changing.

Perhaps some would consider it the height of parochialism to believe that women of the present day lead lives that are more complex and burdensome, spiritually speaking, than those of the women of any other time. But that is precisely what I do in fact believe and what I hope this book may illustrate. The women who scratched the earth in the Plymouth Colony must have lived with fears and uncertainties we cannot even imagine, and just to think of the hardships of the women who traveled west for months and months with their men and children and households in those long-ago covered wagons is to marvel at the human capacity for sheer loyalty and guts. None of us today, I think, could even come near them. But there is one burden that these women were not required to carry—a burden that in its way seems to me the greatest of all: that is, it was never stipulated by the culture around them that they had to assume the responsibility for providing themselves with something that could be adjudged a rich and fulfilling life.

As it happens, when we are left to our own devices, as most of us have been brought up to be, such a responsibility is an impossibly heavy one to shoulder. Without a great deal of luck and a great deal of help from others—an idea that actually violates the terms of what the culture teaches us—we are almost certain to fail.

I myself have spent, or rather wasted, a certain amount of my time on earth under the influence of the notion that a truly successful woman is someone able to insure her own continuing well-being, however she herself has defined it; and I observe women all around me—from the ages of eighteen to eighty, each after her own kind—doing precisely the same.

That is why I have made so bold as to tell my story. The particulars are naturally mine alone, but I cannot help believing that many of the experiences I have to tell about—including much of the foolishness—may underneath it all seem comfortingly familiar: to girls growing up, to their mothers, and most certainly to their grandmothers.

Hopefully, too, it will offer a bit of inside enlightenment to the men who love them and wish so desperately to understand what it is that they are up to.

An Old Wife's Tale

❧ 1 ❧

Oh, What a Lovely War

MY MOTHER AND FATHER had three daughters. This was a circumstance, we children often heard it said, that my father did not mind in the least; on the contrary, my mother and he would smilingly insist, three daughters would one day bring him the happiness of having three sons-in-law. This was said so often, indeed, as to become suspect even to me, the youngest and hence by rights the most credulous member of the family. Will it surprise anyone to be told that when the time came, my father was in the end barely able to maintain civil relations with any of his sons-in-law?

My mother, before the weight of getting on in years began to stoop her shoulders, was a tall woman, one of three tall sisters, and, as it would turn out, taller than any of her daughters. She was also very nearly omnicompetent, with an overweening sense of duty. The youngest of ten siblings, she was left in her

early teens in charge of the family household and of her old and
ailing mother, and this experience clearly made its mark on all
of her life. She did everything competently: cooked for multi-
tudes, ran a household that continued to be a kind of gathering
place for her scattered siblings, was a leader in several communal organizations, was a devoted and successful fund-raiser—
and, until she was no longer needed, she also worked with my
father in his business.

One of my sisters and I would sometimes complain to her
that she was never at home the way this one's or that one's
mother was. But looking back on it, I have come to the surprising conclusion that had she in addition to everything else
been dutifully on hand with the milk and cookies every afternoon, it would have been an even trickier proposition to grow
up in her shadow.

My father, at least before the process of growing old began
to sour it (and except where his sons-in-law were involved),
had a naturally cheerful and even playful disposition. It was he
who provided the children's entertainment, out in the snow
with us in winter and at the lake in summer. It was he who
enjoyed sitting at the dinner table, or standing by the family
piano, and singing. And it was he who could take a tease. As a
result, many outsiders had the impression that my mother was
the one who, as they said then, "wore the pants." But nothing
could have been farther from the truth. Despite her endless
displays of strength, family decisions were always as he made
them, and things were always as he desired them to be. Sum-
merhouses, for example—on a lake only forty-five minutes
from my hometown, St. Paul, Minnesota—were bought,
sold, bought, sold, and built all by him and all according to his
desires and specifications; and as my mother got older and
more and more easily tired, the houses over which he had

decided she was to preside seemed to get bigger rather than smaller.

After she died in her late seventies, when like most elderly widowers he could not manage to live alone, he married a woman who completely reversed the direction of power in the household. She trotted him around, demanded everything of him, sometimes patronized him, and they quarreled and quarreled—which seemed not to be too injurious to him at that, though it was painful for his daughters to watch, because in the end he lived to be ninety-two and died most gracefully.

Of the three of us daughters, I, as the last-born, came the closest to being a kind of honorary son. What I mean by this is that somehow more was expected of me and at the same time I was given a longer leash. To some extent this little extra measure of latitude must have been the result of the fact that, even in the most well-driven of households, by the time the youngest child arrives, the regimen is bound to slacken: the spirit is strong but the flesh weakens. But I am certain that the lessening of the starch in my early upbringing also had to do with my having represented the last disappointed hope for a boy.

In any case, there was always a certain note of turbulence— "rein her in" and "let her go"—in even my earliest childhood memories. I must have been annoyingly talkative, for example, because my mother often used to refer to me with the Yiddish word for "mouth." It was an expression half of pride, talking being a true mark of achievement in Jewish children, and half of disapproval, because I didn't seem to "know my place." And as the years wore on, there got to be more and more of the latter and less and less of the former.

St. Paul was then a city large enough to contain far-off neighborhoods that one might never set foot in and small enough to impose the demand to conduct oneself as all one's neighbors do. My mother was born in St. Paul; my father came there to make his fortune, so to speak, at the age of seventeen. They met through their common interest in Zionism, became engaged, and when my father returned from the army in World War I, they were married and settled there permanently. My mother had a small inheritance from her parents, hardly enough to buy a kid a car these days, and my father lost all of it on his first business deal. But he kept going, and later on, in the years after World War II, made it back with huge interest.

My earliest childhood was spent in Depression time and Roosevelt time. As far as the Depression was concerned, there must have been a serious pinch in our household, as there was everywhere, but I certainly didn't feel it. Having been two years old when the stock market collapsed and the economy began to grind to a halt, I was too young to experience any difference in the world around me and could only know what I overheard.

My father in those years had a little store where he sold mainly workingmen's clothes and what he called "outdoor apparel," which included such items as snowsuits and hunting outfits. My mother, as I said, worked with him there, and we had a live-in maid. This, by the way, was not extraordinary where I grew up, even in the heart of the Depression: the housemaids were young girls from the farms not far outside of the city who were paid God-knows-what and were just grateful to have escaped into town, where at least on their Thursday nights off they could have a little fun. We had two such maids over the course of about twelve years; each got married and left us. Being the baby, I was the one most closely tied to them, and it was from the second of them, for example, a girl called Rose, that I learned about sex.

We also knew that the Depression was making a lot of

people very poor because my mother kept reminding us of it, especially when we didn't wish to eat the food that we found on our plates. And one day I heard talk among the adults about how a certain family down the street were, as they called it then, "on relief." I used to play with their children and knew that "on relief" was something bad because I had been cautioned in hushed tones that the family felt humiliated by it and I wasn't to mention the subject. Anyway, everybody understood that as soon as President Roosevelt saved the country, people would quickly be off this thing it was so shameful to be "on."

In my late teens, when I moved to New York and became a passionate moviegoer, I saw all those images of the Depression that I had somehow missed by living in my Middle Western cocoon: breadlines and shanty towns and little boys riding the rails and hoboes begging door to door (if any had come to our door, it would surely have been kept secret from me on the grounds that such things are not for the innocent eyes of little children).[1]

Though we were far from rich, the lateness of my education about what the Depression had really done to people no doubt sounds like the parochialism of the well-off; and where I lived, there was certainly enough parochialism to go all around and then some. But in those days there was something else to engage my family's attention. A new worry was beginning to take precedence in our consciousness, and that was the growing threat from a man named Adolf Hitler in a distant land called

---

1. I also read a good deal of the literature of the Depression, novels and especially plays, and thereby experienced my first real case of cognitive dissonance: these works were about things unrelievedly grim, but judging from the music of their tone, their authors seemed to be having the time of their lives writing them.

Germany against people like us, namely, Jews. It was in the
mind of the seven-, eight-, and nine-year-old me, a Jewish girl
growing up in the American heartland, that Germany seemed a
far-away land. My father had been in Germany with the
United States Army in World War I, so it was a land that life
had already carried him to—just as its next-door neighbor
Poland was a land life had carried him away from when he was
brought to America while still in his mother's arms. So when
my parents finally helped us to understand that the people this
bad man Hitler was persecuting were "people like us," we were
deeply grateful to be the safe and lucky ones and deeply fearful
at the same time. We sometimes listened on our shortwave
radio to a speech being given by this Hitler, and without our
understanding the words, just from the music of it, we had no
trouble understanding the import. We also sometimes listened
to the Sunday afternoon broadcasts of a man named Father
Coughlin, who used to warn that it was not, as we thought of
them, "people like us" but we Jews ourselves who were among
other dastardly things working to get America's sons killed in a
foreign war.

Beyond our fears of Hitler, the biggest distraction from
whatever anxieties the Great Depression had stirred in the
adults all around me was being provided daily by those two
Roosevelts, Franklin and Eleanor. Could anyone at that moment have been more reassuring, especially to a Jewish family,
than those two? Just to watch newsreels of Mrs. Roosevelt
trotting all over the country in her ugly hats and speaking in
that quality-folks voice made us feel that everything would
soon be in hand. As for her husband, well, surely he was the
wisest, cleverest, bravest, most handsome and charming politician the world had ever seen. (The carrying-on over Jack and
Jackie in 1961 was really small beer compared to the emotions

of the world as I then knew it.) And in my family in particular, there was the added feeling of reassurance—far from justified, as it would turn out in at least one aspect—that when push came to shove, Roosevelt would weigh in and save the Jews.

My mother had a much older sister living in Miami whom we drove down to visit in the summer of 1935. This aunt of mine had a daughter who was a Republican (she would later become a member of the Republican National Committee) and whose husband was a, if not the, leading Republican of Dade County. He was a builder and had just commenced a housing development for poor Negroes in Miami that would many years later turn out to be exactly the opposite of what he had dreamed; i.e., it became one of Florida's worst crime-infested black ghettos. In the car on the way south, there were cautions about how for the sake of having a pleasant visit no one should even mention the word politics. But it turned out that this was a futile hope, since my aunt had been converted by her daughter and was not only a convinced Republican but an obsessive one. Now, in my brief life to that point, I had never even met a Republican and understood little of all that . . . until, to my indescribable shock, my aunt, my mother's own sister, began to inveigh against Roosevelt. She was a pretty good inveigher at that, and I stood frozen as I listened to things I never in my whole eight years could have imagined that anyone would say, let alone my very own aunt, my flesh and blood.

That was the moment when I came to understand there were all sorts of people in the world. This was a revelation. To be sure, in school and on my street I was acquainted with a variety of kids, who attended several different churches in the neighborhood and sometimes had strong and very different opinions from mine about such issues as which was more exciting, *Jack Armstrong, the All-American Boy*—my own favorite

radio series—or *Buck Rogers in the Twenty-fifth Century.* Sometimes, even, the discussion of such differences could get rather
heated and noisy. But that there could be such a thing among
decent people as a Roosevelt-hater, that was different—indeed,
it was my first real taste of the complexity of life.

Not many years later, I would be treated to whole mouthfuls
of complexity. Only then, on the long, slogging journey
through the days and nights of adolescence, my puzzlement
would be, as the man once said, "merely personal." But when it
came to public affairs, Roosevelt had become an essential fixture of our lives, always there, always indispensable, and for
that very reason no longer even necessary to think about: he
would go on being elected president forever, and he would
look after things. (Perhaps if we, young as we were, had known
how very ill he was about to be, we might have viewed him
differently, but the truth is, he had come to seem to us kids to
be simply a permanent, immovable presence.) I find it difficult
to explain this to people who weren't there and who now with
hindsight look upon Roosevelt as a politician who had this
strength and that weakness, had this virtue and that fatal flaw,
pursued this saving policy and created that disaster. (I would
one day many, many years later come to have friends who had
been brought up to believe that Roosevelt was the devil incar-
nate, and in this particular respect their childhoods seem as interesting and curious to me as if they had grown up on Easter
Island.) For us, even more than a hero, which he certainly and
most grandly was, Roosevelt was a fact of nature.

And then came something whose impact is even harder to
talk about with people who weren't around at the time: World
War II. For one thing, by the time the United States was offi-
cially a military participant in it, on December 7, 1941, the war
had already become both a romantic and a real part of my life

and the lives of all my friends and relatives—everyone in my world, in fact. In our view, only a fantasist or a really bad person could ever have imagined that we should stay out of the war. We saw newsreels of rallies being held by America First, a group of people who on various grounds were fighting for America to stay neutral, and those people might just as well have been aliens living on the moon. And to top it off, I was Jewish and growing ever more fervently so with each bit of news about what the Nazis were doing to people like me. America's joining in the fighting, then, was for me in addition to everything else a kind of vicarious revenge.

Furthermore, that the country was almost totally unprepared, as the destruction wreaked on the U.S. Navy by the bombing of Pearl Harbor so clearly illustrated, only made the great race to rearm all the more thrilling. A thousand tanks a month Mr. Roosevelt had called for, along with I no longer remember how many planes and ships, and what followed was what seemed to us, and in fact was, a kind of industrial miracle. Everywhere people were putting their shoulders to the wheel and—to add to the cheer—were at long last making good money doing it.

All of this we could see with our eyes in the newsreels that in those days accompanied the showing of every movie. Of course, for people who can view newscasts for twenty-four hours a day, ten minutes or so of newsreel shown before a movie must seem like a quaint curiosity. But especially during the war, those snippets about the week's events narrated by some unseen and unforgettably plummy voice, weren't really intended to inform us so much as they were both to cheer us up and to egg us on. Moreover, they worked: even in this jaded time, some people might still find it thrilling to be given a bird's-eye view of acres and acres and acres of American tanks and planes hot off the production line with all sorts of smiling workers sitting on top of them and cheering. There were also newsreels of the war itself, and they, too, were intended to make the viewer feel that everything was going as it should: more tanks, this time with smiling and waving soldiers rather than workers sitting on top of them, cigarettes dangling from their lips. (Sometimes there would be a clip of a bombing raid over Germany, and I without compunction would cheer the loudest.)

In order to produce as we were doing and at the same time grow the army and navy, as we were also doing, everybody had to participate: women, old men, and even kids, who ran around collecting empty aluminum cans and used tinfoil "for the war effort." Thus was born the legend of Rosie the Riveter, the gallant lady with her hair tied in a bandanna at work bolting down the sides of a ship or plane in California, say, or assembling parts for jeeps in Michigan. She, too, would be the heroine of some newsreel or other, grinning at her labors or standing in the doorway of the plant for a break and a smoke. This made a particularly pleasing, and its way quite enviable, image—though hardworking Rosie would undoubtedly have been astonished at the thought that some thirty years later she would turn up as a kind of icon for educated young women who would deplore the fact that she had been required to take off her bandanna and go back home. For the truth is that when her husband, or boyfriend, or son, returned from the army, while she might miss the jingle of money in her own pockets, she was for the most part relieved to be doing so. For now there was a home to make and a man whom she had missed terribly to make happy and babies to bring into this world.

In the late nineties, the TV anchorman Tom Brokaw published two books about World War II, both of which were big best-sellers. Brokaw had been an army brat during the war, and in his view the men who fought in World War II were the country's "greatest generation." This idea was greeted with wild enthusiasm by a country mightily fed up with both the memory of the national anxiety attack over the war in Vietnam and the anti-Americanism of the country's intellectuals and journalists. Obviously, there isn't and can't be such a thing as a "greatest" generation. The men who fought in World War II were men like any other: good, bad; mean, generous; brave, cowardly; dutiful, cynical. They were, like all soldiers and sailors, men doing what they were told to do. But they were also people being reminded every day, by their military authorities and by the whole civilian population they left behind, that what they were doing was both vitally important and good. They were not the greatest generation of American men, but they were possibly the most beloved (and, if the reception of Tom Brokaw's books means anything, they continue to be).

Anyway, everybody who wanted to be working was, and everybody who was working was saving money, including the men and women in the armed forces. My father's store had expanded to include military stuff (there was an old army fort nearby, now newly activated, and also an army school for teaching Japanese to a selected group of soldiers slated to be in the army of occupation) and his business had grown significantly. Two cousins worked there full-time, along with a lady whose husband had once (in my eyes all romantically) served a little time in jail for playing some part in a long-ago bootlegging operation.[2] I worked there, too, on Thursday nights and Saturdays, and though I sometimes complained that working in

---

2. My hometown happened to be on the truck route between Canada, where during Prohibition it had been legal to make whiskey, and Al Capone's operation in Chicago, and driving for Capone was a source of big money and a lot of danger for the unlucky ones like him.

the store was putting a crimp in my social activities, the truth is I loved it. I loved pretending to be older, though I'm sure I fooled no one, and I loved the achievement of making sales. One of the cousins who worked there was a great big robust woman who sometimes told dirty jokes (or at least they seemed so to me; they were probably quite innocent), and I adored hanging around her. She was also a great, aggressive saleslady, and taught me to understand that once a customer walked out the door without having bought anything, he or she was to be accounted a sale lost forever. One day some years hence when I was truly broke, my early experience as a saleslady stood me in good stead: I marched into the nearest department store and on the strength of my "experience" got myself a temporary job in the bargain slips department.

Meanwhile, of course, I was growing up. Or so, anyway, it certainly seemed to me, ignorant as I was about how far that "up" would have to stretch before I could know myself to be an adult.

The critic (and my onetime boss and dear friend) Robert Warshow once said that an adolescent boy is someone who wakes up one morning to discover that one of his arms is longer than the other and that he has a permanent erection. Well, then, an adolescent girl is someone who can live through all the upheaval of her country's having gone to war—her friends, neighbors, and relatives going off to the army or navy; the bustle of everyone at home's playing some part, even if only a laughable one, in the war effort; the shortage of things like meat and butter and gasoline that had been everyday features of life (and most critically for me and my friends as the years wore on, cigarettes); the early bad news from the fronts

of both Asia and Europe—someone who lives in full consciousness in the midst of all this and at the same time sincerely
worries that her ears are too big or her thighs too fat.

It is probably a toss-up as to who has a harder time of it, the
girls or the boys, each after his or her own kind, in the years
that stretch from fourteen to, say, nineteen. I am told by a variety of people who claim authority in the matter that nowadays
things are different among adolescents. Since girls happily have
been relieved of the need to remain chaste, or even to pretend
to remain chaste, they say, sex is no longer a problem for them;
and with sex eliminated as an issue, the rest of their experience
has become much easier. Well, perhaps; but it certainly doesn't
look much easier to me. I myself believe that easy sex among
the kids has led not to the absence of problems but to a different, and very likely more serious, set of them. Falling casually
into bed, or falling into wherever else it is they have sex, does
not alter the fact that for the girl an entirely different set of
needs is being acted on than for the boy. Current theory may
have it that they have identical sexual natures, but if so, current
theory, as Mr. Bumble said of the law, is "a ass." Be that as it
may, "hooking up" with some boy or boys in any case does
nothing about an adolescent girl's primary preoccupation with
such problems as that her nose is too big or her skin is broken
out or it seems to her she will remain permanently flat-chested.

As for me and my friends, I can tell you that everything having to do with sex was certainly an issue of the greatest interest
and concern to us. Not to be a virgin was a scandal, but to remain chaste was a far from simple proposition. For sex was our
main source of power over the boys who otherwise exerted an
untoward degree of power over us. They and only they had the
capacity to make us popular—O beatific condition—and hence
to give us status. Sought-after as any of us might be among the

girls, to be left uninvited by a boy to certain critical occasions was to feel oneself, justified or not, to be the object of pitiless sniggering. "What do you care?" one's mother might say by way of offering consolation, which only served to underline the futility of relying on her judgment in anything. For adolescents, there is no reasoning with the oppressive weight of community opinion; they know what they know, and anyone who doesn't is simply too obtuse to be trusted.

But when it came to sex, the boys needed us far, far more than we needed them. Call it nature's way of evening the score.

I was the member of a group of girls who were thought by many, among them my mother and father, to be quite bad. I was never exactly punished but was rather treated to an occasional blast of cold and quiet disapproval. I was an intelligent girl, I would be told; I read books and wrote poems and appeared to be serious about many things; why did I not spend my time with other serious girls, like so-and-so or the daughter of her friend so-and-so? If I had needed anything more to plight eternal friendship to each and every one of the unruly members of my own gang, that would certainly have been it.

Anyway, when I think back on what the word "bad" might have connoted, I have to laugh. We did spend a great deal of time hanging out together that might have been far more profitably used, and we were certainly anything but ladylike. Among ourselves, for example, we used a good deal of foul language (though nothing nearly as foul as the language I later became habituated to as a student in a theological seminary in New York). We would cut school now and then, sitting in the neighborhood drugstore puffing on cigarettes and consuming gallons of Pepsi. And we would have pajama parties—usually in the home of one of our friends whose parents were out of town a good deal, at which we would spend much of the time telling dirty jokes and conducting largely abstract discussions on the subject of boys and sex.

Ah, boys and sex.

We did hang out a good deal, though not exclusively, with a particular gang of boys who were our classmates and hence in our view somewhat too young for us. The custom of the country in those days was dating, two by two, couples off by themselves to a dance or a movie or a party and an inevitable tussle in the car on the way home. Dating, however, was something generally done with boys who were older: first, on the theory that females were more "mature" than males, and second, because it was more likely that they would both venture on actual dates and have cars in which to do so. By the same token, formal dating could be something of an iffy proposition, putting us girls at the distinct disadvantage of needing to be asked. Of course, there were always a couple of girls—the class beauty queen or the class tramp—who had no difficulty with the dating system; for the rest of us, though, it was by no means assured that we would have some Saturday night spoken for. This problem was entirely one of status, since there was small assurance that our date, especially the tussle in the car, would make for a happier diversion than hanging out with our girlfriends. Here is where the younger boys came in: they could always be counted on to turn up somewhere as needed and redress the balance. They could serve to help provide a night's entertainment, and they could without too much consequence be toyed with a little.

Thus in exchange for the terrible dependence of adolescent girls on male acknowledgments of their desirability and worth they, of course, could and did make use of the weapon of sex. Here the balance of need against need often led to the most brutal kind of manipulation on both sides. Again, I am told with great assurance by those who claim to know that the new sexual freedom has obviated the need for any struggle whatsoever between the girls and the boys. And again I say perhaps. Since their respective interests are, as they have always been, by nature so different, I continue to permit myself to wonder. As far as we were concerned, at least, the nature of the girl-boy transaction led to the invention of a system that might be called full male sexual arousal without satisfaction. Some of the girls would take this system far enough to get a kind of statement of commitment; others would not succeed so far. The point of the exercise was that the only way to avenge our need for them was to produce material evidence of their need for us. Sometimes, to be sure, a girl would discover that she was less in control of the situation, and of herself, than she had planned on being, and some form of consummation would then take place. This, alas, would violate the whole purpose of the transaction by serving only to increase her dependence on him. Such an event was rare, however, not only because the girls at the last minute would find it quite easy to be resistant but because the boys on their side were usually inhibited by the thought of how much responsibility they could be bringing down upon themselves. I do not believe that a single one of my girlfriends, as they used to say, "got into trouble," but many a tearful scene was nevertheless created.

All this was a dreadful way to run a railroad, no doubt about it. Only two things can be said for it. First of all, none of this exchange was conscious. And second, it certainly did not leave us jaded, or old before our time.

The system of dating I have described naturally began to unravel at the point in life where my friends and I came up against the seriousness of the war in our own lives and began to feel the ever-widening effect of military conscription. The older boys for whom we had so assiduously set our caps were gone; the boys who had been our playmates were themselves champing at the bit to get into the army, or preferably the navy,[3] and one by one they, too, were disappearing. There were those soldiers studying Japanese nearby, but they were for the most part much too worldly and dangerous for the likes of us, and there were some older boys who had for one reason or another not been called up yet, and they were either waiting to be called at any minute or were in our view to be considered objects of either pity or suspicion. Like the soldiers, those who were waiting to be drafted were for the most part hell-bent, sexually speaking, or else they were in a frame of mind to demand some kind of serious commitment, so that when they finally made it into the war they could have "a girl back home." Several times this kind of pressure led to sudden passionate partings, after which the next years were spent in the writing of letters, the exchanging of little gifts and photographs, and daydreaming about engagement and marriage.

Not surprisingly, few of these exchanges and daydreams did in the end lead to marriage, though a couple of my friends actually stuck to their guns and were rewarded with early marriage to their returning veterans. They had also been able to keep their friends supplied with cigarettes from the cartons that were so considerately being sent to them from the army PX. But many more of the girls who had got themselves involved with some new draftee under the pressure of his imminent shipment into harm's way got tired of the routine after a while and simply stopped writing, or perhaps began to correspond with someone else. And last, a few of the girls took up with the

3. The common lore among the boys in those days was that if you were going to get shot at, at least in the navy you had a dry place to sleep and hot meals.

men studying Japanese, pretending to themselves that they were "in love" and soon after nursing broken hearts.

I had a bit of a taste of all these experiences. I dutifully wrote letters—though the ones into which I truly poured my affection were not to a pretend beau but to a beloved cousin, a bombardier who was shot down and killed over Germany—and I even claimed a couple of times to have had my heart broken. But all the time what was really moving in my spirit, and had indeed been moving there since my early childhood, was the desire to leave home and make my way in New York.

My father's family lived in Brooklyn, and when he took me there at age six to see and be seen by all the relatives, I fell in love with the bustle and the smells and the variety of the place, and in all the years after that—up to this very minute, in fact— my feelings have never changed. (I have a young grand-daughter who lives elsewhere and visits from time to time, and I can recognize the same thing now going on in her.)

But by the time I reached late adolescence and my early twenties, something else was churning up in my spirit as well, something I found it difficult—and to this day find it difficult—to talk about without sounding false and self-dramatizing. For with the celebration of the war's end and the return of the soldiers from Europe and the Pacific came word of what the evil Herr Hitler had wrought: six million people like me, ordinary Jews, men, women, children, babies, slaughtered in cold blood—transported from their homes to be starved to death, shot, gassed, reduced to ashes in ovens. I was so enraged I literally did not know what to do with myself. In the years that followed the end of the war books of memoirs about the ghettos and death camps began to appear in print, and I read them all (probably the right way to put it is "inhaled" them all). And from there I moved on to books about the Soviet Gulag.

You might say I became a concentration-camp junkie. Spiritually speaking, I suppose this was not the finest thing on earth to be, but for some years I simply could not stop. Nor could I figure out what to do with the feelings it gave me.

Many years afterward, in the late sixties, my husband and I were invited to join a group that was making a junket to Germany. We were asked to list our requests for things we wished to see while in the country. I put down "a concentration camp" and, I later discovered, thereby caused a good deal of discomfort among our German hosts. But they did arrange for us to visit Dachau—not the worst of the camps, fewer than a quarter of a million were killed there, mostly by shooting, but still there were a couple of gas chambers and ovens in evidence. And after all my reading, I still had something to learn about the Holocaust, that is, the human proportion of it. Jews may have been slaughtered by the millions, but they were burned one by one in those ovens. To begin with, these contraptions were not some fiery cauldron but ordinary ovens of the size a baker might use. Each body was lifted by two men onto a kind of rack and deposited into the flames. Afterward, many people who performed functions like these in the camps pled in self-defense that they had no alternative, that they were merely following orders. To me, standing there in Dachau, it looked as if it would have taken an enormous amount of energy of the kind that only violent hatred could supply to spend one's days lifting human bodies one by one and dumping them into a furnace.

But almost at the same time as I had commenced to bathe myself in the horror that had befallen more than one-third of my fellow Jews, something else was happening to those who had remained alive: a state came into being in the ancient Jewish land in order to guarantee a safe harbor for any Jew anywhere in the world. The struggle to declare the independent existence of this Jewish land had been going on for nearly a century; my parents, as I said, had met in the Zionist movement and had later devoted a good deal of their time and energy in the effort of Zionists to convince the world that the Jews not only needed a sanctuary but had the historic right to claim the land called Palestine for their own. And after the Holocaust the civilized countries of the world relented and voted to give the Jews at least a part of that land, after which the State of Israel, that over the years would find itself under an almost relentless series of military attacks, brought to safety the Jews still left in European camps, the Jews of Arab lands, of Romania, of Ethiopia, and finally of Soviet Russia. Between the Holocaust and the existence of the State of Israel, I found myself (in this I must have been like hundreds of thousands of others) down and up and down again in a state of high emotion over the course of some years. I once kicked an old friend out of my house after inviting him for dinner because he had become a pacifist and was on that occasion preaching that since we all bear responsibility for violence in the world, we must forgive the Germans.

But all that would reach its peak of highest intensity sometime in the future. Meanwhile there was a private fantasy to fulfill: that life in New York, which I had never ceased to long for. As it happened, my parents took it for granted that when my sisters and I finished college we would almost surely leave home to seek our fortune. Not everyone in our world did that, but many did. On leaving college, each of my two older sisters left for the excitement of wartime Washington; one remained, and eventually married there, and one, no lover of hubbub, returned to the quieter comforts of home. What was different in my case was that I had not finished college; on the contrary, I had dropped out.

I'm not sure to this day that I know why I did that. Perhaps if I had ever had a shrink he could have told me. I certainly promised to be a more than adequate student, and I must have known somewhere way at the back of my mind that it would cause me difficulty in the future not to have a college degree. All I could figure is that at that point in my life there must have been some deep desire in me to fail.

I had never ceased being keen to get out of town. As a senior in high school, for instance, I had wanted to go to the University of Chicago. But that was not on, as the British say, having been regarded by my parents as "unnecessary." So I dropped out of the University of Minnesota, two miles from my home, and once again plotted to get away. Through all my years of elementary and junior high school, I had studied Hebrew in after-school classes, four days a week and Sunday. And now—whether to my parents' chagrin or relief it would be hard to say, but at least with their helpless approval—I was off to New York to perfect my Hebrew at the College of Jewish Studies of the Jewish Theological Seminary of America and otherwise, as the cliché of the time would have it, "find myself."

My heart lifted so high as I boarded that train that some years would pass before it came back down again.

Leaving home seemed quite natural, not only to me but to the whole community in which I had grown up. In my husband's family, I would learn, such a departure from home would have been regarded as absolutely out of the question. Worse than out of the question, it could only signal one thing: the intent on the part of a daughter to be a whore or of a son to be a bum. There was only one legitimate way to escape maternal overlordship, and that was to be married. I sometimes used to wonder what would have become of me if I had had to grow up under such a dispensation, and the answer unmistakably was: nothing good, for sure.

More than fifty years later, I am still capable now and then of feeling the same excitement mixed with relief I felt then at the thought that I was really and truly living in New York.

I would in only a little more than a year have come to be married to my first husband and to serve as the classic older married friend to a young student who would a decade later, to the amazement of both of us, be my second—and forevermore.

And thereby hangs the tale of my life as a woman in that decade of recent and fateful ill repute, the 1950s.

2

My Blue Heaven

MY FIRST MARRIAGE, like that of millions of other women, was to a veteran completing his education on the GI Bill. This happened less than two years after I had settled in New York, and I can't really imagine what we lived on to begin with: it must have been—or rather have been the illusion of—love. He was in school, and the government was giving him ninety dollars a month through the GI Bill. Between us we were making another hundred or so teaching Sunday school. There must have been some other source of income, but what it could have been I can't for the life of me remember. Anyway, we first moved into a furnished room with what they called a "galley" kitchen, bathroom down the hall, in the heart of a Brooklyn slum. Our housing obviously cost very little, but still we had to eat and pay subway fares and go to an occasional movie. Moreover, the theory was that he was to go on from his bachelor's degree to a doctorate, so that he could one day get a job teaching in a university. This was a sensible plan: since with the huge expansion of the student body in those postwar years—millions of former GIs taking advantage of their government's generosity either to go for the first time or go back to college—such jobs were not only plentiful but seemed to us and to everyone we knew to be eminently desirable. The three, or maybe four, years spent in penury before he could earn a real living, then, would be well spent.

I was supposed to be going to school as well, but that, as anyone who knew me could see, was an absurd idea. I kept saying, "What would happen if either of us were to break a leg or need an operation?" The obvious answer was that I would leave school and get myself a job. You might think this involved some kind of sacrifice on my part, but to be honest (something I rarely was in those days), this whole line of argument was a charade, played in order to give myself an air of virtue. The truth was that, in New York no less than in my hometown, I simply hated going to school.

After all, had I wished to remain a student, there was such a thing as part-time work; we could both have found some and added to the family coffers that way. But I was both pleased and relieved not to have to be a student anymore.

That was one part of the charade; another part was that but for one lone semester of typing in high school, I had not even the pretense of a proper marketable skill. So hearing that I was looking for work, a friend of my husband's who was the executive director of a youth organization took me on as a clerk, for what was a joke of a salary. Aside from all those Thursday nights and Saturdays at my father's store, my first job. I loved it. There were a young and a not-so-young girl working in the office, and I enjoyed their company and listened avidly to their life stories, especially their respective complaints about the men, or lack of same, in their lives. We did a little bit of everything in that office, and I became a whiz at folding, stuffing into envelopes, sealing, and stamping the hundreds upon hundreds of letters that were sent out in our frequent mass mailings. (This may sound like, and I suppose in a way was, the bottom of the bottom of clerical jobs, but it would turn out that my skill as a mailing assistant was to stand me in very good stead on more than one occasion in my future professional life.)

Love it as I might, though, the pay was ludicrous. So off I went on the climb: a job that was a little better than that, followed by another that was better than the second, and so on, all the while acquiring enough experience with the typewriter to give me hope that I might one day find myself in a place that truly contented me. And so it was that after two and a half years of wandering, I landed at a magazine called *Commentary,* a relatively new highbrow Jewish magazine, where I was to be secretary to the managing editor. My typing was just enough above hopeless for him to tolerate it (though not entirely without grumbling) and I simply could not believe my luck in finding myself there.

Many years later, when I was the executive editor of *Harper's* magazine, I was invited to meet with a group of young women at Yale who were interested in going into publishing. I was familiar with the experience of talking to such girls because each June an army of new graduates just like them descended on the magazine, as well as on every book publishing house in New York, looking for the great job that would lead them to those mythical Manhattan cocktail parties and into the circle, if not the bed, of some famous writer. They knew little of the world, and had had no experience of working, even in a five-and-dime. A very little gentle probing on my part would then result in the revelation that it was actually my job they were applying for! So I arrived at Yale knowing full well the kind of information about publishing these girls would be seeking from me. Now, this was only the second or third year that girls had been accepted into Yale, and they had been the crème de la crème of American high-school students, but that only made my certainty about what they wanted of me all the greater. The first question asked me was, what had I needed to get my first break in—sigh—publishing. "Ah," I answered, "I knew how to type!" For all intents and purposes that ended the session; they were too outraged to say another word—though if they had asked half the women executives then in the publishing business, they could have gotten the same answer.

As far as *Commentary* was concerned, while it was true that I had not managed to stay in school, it happened that I was far from illiterate, and there were services I could perform that seemed to compensate for my stenographic shortcomings. I established a consistent system for transliterating Hebrew, for example, and I several times caught what might have been embarrassing errors in biblical citation. I could do triage on what in magazine parlance is so elegantly called "the slush pile," namely, unsolicited manuscripts. And in general I was interested, truly interested, in the common enterprise—which was by itself worth something in a secretary.

What made me happiest of all, however, is that in this office I found people who not only told me their stories, as had my first office mates, but some of whom were to become my lifelong friends. My boss, Robert Warshow, was one of them, as were two other young editors named Nathan Glazer and Irving Kristol. And then there was Sherry Abel, hired about six months after me to be the editorial assistant (in that office the editorial assistant was the person mainly in charge of production). One morning in Sherry walked—hair tied in a ponytail, big long skirt, sandals, all Greenwich Village standard issue—said something and laughed, and for me it was love at first sight. We lived very near to one another, and we used to go home together after work every day, sometimes walking, sometimes on the bus, and sometimes, sinfully, in a taxi.

Sherry was an extraordinary woman: a dyed-in-the-wool bohemian who was capable of making the most wonderful fun of various aspects of her own bohemianism, such as her long string of food fads, and who had an enduring passion for good writing, painting, and elevated wit. There was nothing one needed to fear talking to her about, and there was nothing she feared saying about herself. Her friendship added immeasurably to the pleasures of my life. (Years later, she would find herself working for my future husband, which somehow put a small crimp in our relationship, for it was as if she became his and ceased to be mine.)

I would leave *Commentary* in the sixth month of my first pregnancy. As it happens, I would be back there again, but that is getting ahead of my story. In any case, after all my maneuvering, my first husband and I had "come up" in the world and were by now living on a quiet leafy street in Greenwich Village. Our apartment, a third-floor walk-up, was what they used to call a railroad flat—all rooms off a single corridor. Rumor had it that the building had originally been put up as a tenement, with a communal bathroom on each floor, but by the time we moved into it, bathrooms had long been installed, one to an apartment. We also had two and a half bedrooms, and paid a rent of seventy dollars a month. I was twenty-three years old.

My pregnancy had been unplanned, but I was very pleased by it, and after a brief time spent in wiping away my tears and accustoming himself to the idea of the new responsibility, my husband was pleased too—or at least professed himself to be so. By that point, he had basically finished most of his course requirements, and the need to put off the writing of his doctoral dissertation for a while and take a job may not have been an altogether unwelcome development.

Enter my mother, center stage right; and with my mother, though I of course didn't recognize it in those terms, enter the famous 1950s. And thereby hangs a tale, or perhaps it should be called a countertale.

Like many of the members of my generation, I came from a relatively small and widely spaced family. (While my mother had been the youngest of ten, I had been the youngest of three, with intervals of more than three years between us.) The Depression had clearly been a condition hostile to the bounteous making of babies. The point is, I myself had spent no time in proximity to babies and had no idea of what they really needed in the way of living arrangements. My mother, however, had many such ideas, and the first of them was that of course I could not possibly have a baby in that Greenwich Village apartment: it was too old and dirty, and there was no way I could manage walking up three flights of stairs with a baby in tow.

Now, that particular moment in American history—the baby was born right after the new year of 1951—was famously the time of a terrible housing shortage. Nothing had been built during the war, and many newly married couples had found themselves stuck for a while in the household of one of their parents, an arrangement hardly conducive to happy days. Another possibility was for them to take up residence in one of the communities ("camps" would have been a better word for it) of Quonset huts rescued by the government from military use and slapped up here and there to serve as living quarters for veterans and their families—sometimes three or four to a hut. In short, we had been very lucky to have found a both livable and affordable apartment in the city, and now, it seemed, we would be required to give it up and plunge more fully into the life of our generation.

In the previous two or three years a few housing projects had commenced construction way out beyond the city where land was still cheap and plentiful. The style of housing in these projects was called "garden" apartments, meaning that the buildings were two stories high, one apartment up and one down. Each unit, consisting of eight or ten apartments, was the equivalent of a city block in length with a little patch of grass stretching along the front. And these projects were massive, stretching for acres and acres, sometimes as far as half a mile each. The economic principle of this new kind of housing seemed to be that for every five miles closer to the heart of the city the rent increased by twenty to thirty dollars a month and the closets got smaller and fewer. As it happened, the apartment we eventually found, nearly an hour out of Manhattan, was still rather more expensive than the rent we had been paying and was a little smaller. But it was brand-new, fixtures all shiny, and as far as my mother was concerned, it fit the bill perfectly.

You might well ask why I should have placed myself under my mother's tutelage in this way—seeing as how I had not done so about anything since the age of fourteen—and especially with respect to such an important decision as where to live. What I said at the time was that I knew absolutely nothing about what was now to befall me and I therefore had to be advised by someone who was so much more experienced. But this was no more than the kind of rationalization reached for by people who are simply afraid and unable to admit being so.

What was I afraid of? Growing up? Leaving the unreality of our make-believe student life where nothing truly decisive could happen? Whatever the reason, tearing myself about as far away as possible from the world in which I had come to be totally at ease and taking myself to the suburbs was the move I had without much resistance agreed to make. In the end, being temporary, it turned out not to be such a bad one. Though hardly necessary, to put it mildly, for the welfare of my baby (soon to be two babies, born a year apart), it did turn out in its way to be entertaining—rather like my first job—and it taught me a couple of very, very important things.

By the 1960s the word "suburbs" came to conjure images of nice houses and trees and greenery, of mothers zipping around in station wagons taking their children to school, or to after-school activities, or to visit friends, and enjoying afternoon card games or shopping at a nearby mall. There is another image of it as well, of course, the one made famous, one might even say indelible, by Betty Friedan: as a society in which women were systematically excluded from the interesting and important lives being led by their husbands, who all unfeelingly hopped aboard a magic train every morning and headed for the Emerald City.

Well, Glen Oaks Village—for such was the name of the project in which I was to spend nearly four years—was certainly a daytime community of women, but with nary a station wagon in sight. Most of our husbands did go to work in the city, all right, after a journey consisting of a forty-minute bus ride followed by a twenty-minute subway ride, and what they did there for the most part was sweat to make a buck. (As it happened, my husband had found himself a relatively pleasant if exceedingly modest job with the federal government. He did not exactly sweat, then, but he trekked for more than an hour on public transit, along with the rest of our neighbors.) Such cars as were to be found mostly belonged to the men who were salesmen, the majority of whom worked on a commission basis and thus had good weeks and bad ones, who dressed what seemed to us expensively in order to keep up appearances, and returned home every night with anxiety sounding from their very footfalls. The rest worked here and there, some more hopefully than others, and returned home each day to find wives who had also been working hard and were tired and in need of them.

Life was certainly far from hopeless for the men of Glen Oaks, though there were nights when you might have thought it was. It was just that they were all starting out in their jobs or careers—thanks to the war a few years behind—and before they could come up for air, they all had a couple of kids. For the war that had put them behind in their working lives had also left them with the need, no doubt mostly unconscious, to plant some new life around themselves. Contraception was certainly not difficult to come by, nor was any of my neighbors in need of instruction in how to use it; but having children at that historic moment was utterly taken for granted as a good thing to do. And the babies in turn kept most of the denizens of Glen Oaks Village more preoccupied than their circumstances had yet entitled them to be with such things as how to afford and where to buy a nice house.

Indeed, the future buying of houses was a steady source of conversation in Glen Oaks; it created the possibility of sociability among men who might otherwise have had little or nothing to say to one another. At the same time, the idea of having to undertake yet another burden made them anxious and sometimes very unpleasant to their wives, who were, after a tiring day with the children, sometimes ready to be quite unpleasant in return. (Even I, who only longed to be able to move back to

Manhattan some day, gave house hunting a brief whirl: it seemed the sociable thing to do, to find out what you could get for how much money in what community.)

A few years ago, a very clever young man named Michael Kinsley, who was then an editor at *The New Republic,* wrote a column in that magazine which first made me laugh and then made me feel very, very weary. Kinsley, a member of the baby boom generation, was complaining that whereas his father had had a very nice house in which to raise his family, real estate values were now so impossibly high that he, Michael, could barely afford even a minimally decent apartment. I did not know Kinsley *père* but I remember very vividly what it took for a man to get his family under a nice roof—how much work and how much worry and how much climbing up that ladder. There was pleasure in it, too, of course, but primarily the pleasure of feeling that one had done right by one's kids. It seemed not to have occurred to Mr. Kinsley *fils* that his father might now and then have dreamed of being footloose in a somewhat shabby apartment of the kind his son was now complaining about.

None of this is intended to suggest that life was not just as hard for the women who were my neighbors and companions. Nor in all the quarrels that one heard through the paper-thin walls that betokened the speed and cheapness of so much of that early postwar construction did one hear a husband accuse a wife of having done nothing all day. Mainly a husband's complaint against his wife was only that she had failed to be sufficiently sympathetic to his troubles. As it happened, our apartment abutted the apartment of a couple who quarreled every night. She was a very pretty kid, not more than twenty-two, and already had three little ones—bing, bing, bing—and he was not much older. They clearly didn't know what had hit them: one day they were necking on a blanket at Jones Beach, and the next they were stuck in four small rooms with three babies. Just feeding them took up most of her day, and he had had to settle for a job that kept him under the thumb of a boss he considered a sadist. I could not help feeling sorry for them both, but this, I quickly discovered, was not a feeling shared by any of the other women in our little corner of the complex, who spent virtually every afternoon gossiping as they sat together watching their tots playing in the grass. Their very sound and very heartless view of the matter was that everybody had made his or her own bed to lie in.

These afternoon sessions were a major form of entertainment. A couple of families among us already had televisions, but they were certainly not for watching in the daytime while the children were awake and in need of fresh air and exercise. Anyway, the truth is that we all found our afternoon gatherings indispensable. One of the things that made it so easy for everyone to talk freely was that we had too little in common to become intimate friends: our social life, such as it was, was led at night. And another thing that kept us comfortable was the knowledge that this place we were living in was merely a way station on a journey that all of us would sooner or later be making to someplace else.

In 1956 W. H. Whyte published a very famous and influential book called *The Organization Man*. In it, he described what he believed to be a decisive new type of social phenomenon, the middle-level corporate executive. This organization man was someone whose life was entirely bound up in and directed by the conditions and rules for advancement in the corporation for which he worked. The suburb in which he lived (for of course he lived in a suburb), the way he dressed and conducted himself and spent his free time, even the kind of woman he married, could either add to or detract from his future prospect for moving up the corporate ladder. In short, he was the wholly owned creature of the organization. Fatefully for the next two decades of American culture, Mr. Whyte's theory was enthusiastically taken up by intellectuals and journalists who wished to shoot down the postwar American economy before they saw the whites of its eyes.[1] In any case, I could not recognize a single friend or neighbor, then or even later—when I would come to know a number of people working in large corporations—in Whyte's book.

The woman who lived upstairs from me was our unacknowledged social leader, and hence most of our gatherings took place on and around the little stoop that served as the entranceway to both our front doors. It's hard to know what makes a particular member of a group its leader; social psychologists have no doubt spent millions of dollars in grants to ponder this question, and I certainly don't know how the lady named Leila, married to a man called Duke and a mother of two, came to be ours. She was very lively and very amusing, and she was certainly the most stylish woman among us, but there was some other kind of authority attaching to her that I can't explain. Anyway, the proximity of her front door to mine turned out for me to be a happy circumstance. I had belonged to a gang of young girls in St. Paul, but I had never hung out in that same fashion with a group of grown women. Aside from helping me through the long afternoons, what this experience

---

1. Nor was Whyte the only author being handsomely rewarded for such fearful images of the lives of his contemporaries. There was, for instance, "the man in the gray flannel suit," the eponymous hero of a best-selling novel and hit movie who had enslaved himself to an advertising agency. Moreover, barely had people begun to mail in their first mortgage payments on their new fifties-style ranch houses than out came another book of pop sociology called *The Crack in the Picture Window.*

was to teach me—as no other experience in my life had done or would ever do—is just how many different kinds of lives there can be even in one small American community. One of us, for instance, had during the war been a B-girl hanging out in Times Square; she was married to a former sailor whom she had picked up there and who adored her. Another was a well-bred girl related to a very famous and distinguished federal jurist who was desperately trying in the midst of all of us to hang on to her sense of being someone of superior background. Still another was a southern beauty with two fairly grown children whose second husband, the children's step-father, was a traffic controller at a nearby airport. Finally, there was a fat and noisy girl who had grown up in the Bronx and who, while she was generally very good-natured as fat and noisy girls from the Bronx tended to be, was in a constant state of angry agitation with my poor little next-door neighbor, she of the perpetually short temper and three babies (who rarely, by the way, came to sit with us).

We were all in pretty much the same boat where the chil-dren were concerned: none of us had been more than distantly connected to babies before our own were born, and we were all sworn to bringing them up more liberally than we ourselves had been brought up. Some of us depended on the experts' books, others did not, but no baby, for instance, was allowed to cry at night, none was thwarted in the desire to suck his thumb, and none was toilet-trained by the age of one. (All of this must sound elementary to young mothers of today, but we ourselves, as we heard over and over from our own mothers, had not been treated with such laxity.) Outside, the children were pretty much given free rein, with their safety being guar-anteed when necessary by our jumping up and chasing after them. Our afternoon chat sessions, then, were not exactly quiet and continuous; still, one way and another, a good deal of amusement was provided and a good deal also got communicated.

It might not come as a surprise to hear that many times the main topic of conversation on that front stoop was husbands. And I do not mean husbands in general but this one's husband and that one's husband very much in particular. As it happened, I made no contribution of my own to that line of conversation: I was far too snooty to do so—and perhaps also too afraid of what I might hear myself say. But I was without question a fascinated auditor. It's not that my playmates were really hostile to their husbands; had they been, listening to them would never have been so diverting. But one day as I was listening, it came to me that I was witnessing the same phenomenon I had once known in high school. It was the old game of sexual power. All day they were being of service—to their children, of course, and, in keeping the home fires burning, to their husbands as well. But at night in their bedrooms it was they who had the upper hand, and they knew it.

Sometimes, baby-sitters being rare and by our lights expensive, a group of us of an evening would trade off going to the movies with our husbands. These expeditions could be great fun—just getting out of the house without elaborate planning was a treat—and led to a good deal of adolescent chatter about the attractions of this or that male star. One afternoon after such an excursion, Leila's mother had come to visit and was taking part in our stoop chatter, during which we arrived at the general consensus that Clark Gable was hands down the one we liked best. "You like, you like," she muttered unforgettably, "look what you married."

Many of the toddlers we were chasing after on those long-ago afternoons would, of course, one day grow up to accuse us all of being bourgeois, conformist, and materialistic. And each time as I would sigh with weariness or grow angry at the sheer ingratitude of it all, I would have to laugh as well, thinking of those days on Leila's stoop. As I would when the feminists came along to declare that our husbands had been oppressive, if not indeed violent, and had trotted far off to the city every day in order to hoard all the goodies for themselves. Some oppressive. Some goodies.

It may or may not come as a surprise to learn that as soon as it was feasible—which is to say, as soon as an affordable apartment turned up—we moved back to Manhattan, only one block away from Central Park in a largely Hispanic neighborhood that in twenty-five years' time would become the very center of yuppie fashion. There were four of us now, and while this new apartment was not exactly grand, it seemed like a palace to me. We could invite friends for dinner, for instance, and it would be easy for them to come. We could walk down the street and see shops and crowds and all different kinds and shades of people. (It has long been my theory that the island of Manhattan, for those who can afford it, is the very best place on earth in which to raise children; just going to the store can be an interesting experience.)

Nor might it be all that surprising for someone to hear that before too long the return to Manhattan would put paid to my marriage. It's always hard to explain truthfully, even to oneself, why one wishes to dump one's marriage, especially when to the naked eye there seems to be no drastic difficulty. Though divorce would soon enough become fairly unremarkable among my friends, formally speaking I was the first in the crowd and was called upon more than once to explain myself, which I in truth found it difficult to do. One day I encountered an old acquaintance, someone with whom years earlier I had taught Sunday school, and on hearing that I had broken up my marriage, he dolefully asked, "Doesn't anyone want to lead the life of quiet desperation any more?" In a way, he had come the closest to the point. Years later I would write an essay on the subject in which I would observe that divorce begins in that moment when one looks into the mirror and says, "Is *this* all there is going to be forever?"

How did moving back to the city bring on such a moment for me? To this day I'm not sure; perhaps it had to do with the fact that New York is a place positively throbbing with possibility. Why otherwise would so many kids just out of school flock here—as I myself had once done—to seek their fortune? Such a thought provides no vindication for the hurt I caused; I have never ceased to be well aware of that. But on the other hand, I would be lying if I denied that I regard it as having saved my own life.

The experts now tell us that divorcing their father was the very worst thing I could have done to my two very small daughters. And I have no way of comparing the fortunes of these children as they turned out with what they might have been. Anyway, after the first stormy arguments my husband and I went through the usual arrangements: so much child support, so much visitation, etc., vowing as people always do—and always in vain—that we would be civilized. My husband moved out, to an apartment not all that far away, and I remained in my shabby four-room palace by the park.

And thus my return to *Commentary,* this time to serve as secretary to the editor in chief. For of course, I now had to support myself, and to some extent my children, too. They say that God looks after drunks and little children. Well, he certainly looked after me, for first crack off the bat I found a Russian lady who had just lost a job and desperately needed another to look after the children. She fancied herself a governess, and always left the house at night considerably dirtier than she had found it. Moreover, she was the world's worst cook, and I think she drove the girls crazy with the way she nagged them to eat. But she would have died for them. So off I trotted to the office each day, feeling more cheerful than I had felt for years.

My boss was a manic depressive who would one day land in a hospital and subsequently take his own life, and he was famous in the intellectual world for being impossible to deal with, but he and I had not a drop of trouble between us. In the winter he was high and in the summer he was low, and in either case he had great difficulty managing details. I had known him from my previous stint at the magazine, so now, as his secretary, I was able to help smooth out his daily existence. My typing was still wanting, and my stenography virtually nonexistent, but he would dictate correspondence to me, I would scribble down the gist of it, and then I would simply write his letters for him. If he ever caught on—and he was an extremely intelligent man—he made no mention of it. Now and then I would stop him from committing some folly, such as insulting an old friend, or being brutal to one of the authors on whom he particularly depended. And in the summers when he got really low, I helped him to pretend he was keeping busy by bustling in and out of his office a good deal.

Two of my friends from my first stint of duty at *Commentary* had left, Nat Glazer for a university, and Irving Kristol for London—where he became coeditor of *Encounter* magazine—but there were two left, Robert Warshow and Sherry, with whom, if anything, I would become even closer. So for me every day felt like going to a small but very exclusive party. Only a little more than a year later, however, Warshow would be dead of a heart attack at the age of thirty-seven, and soon after that, my present boss would grow so paralyzed with depression that he would be taken away to a hospital. There was still work for me to do, however, in a way more than ever, because we were now shorthanded, and the theory was that my boss would return to the office one day soon. He didn't do so, at least not until for the happiest of reasons I was remarried, back at home, and tending to two more babies.

But I get ahead of my story.

The attack against all those men who were working to support their wives and families with jobs in big corporations was the beginning of a more general assault in the culture against the way ordinary Americans had come to live in the postwar world. I myself may not have wished to settle permanently in some freshly built community of nice homes far from the center of town, but most people did. With this new life came a whole new set of habits and choices, and the sense that they would be more at ease after wartime tension and cramping: there would be neighbors and neighborliness and civic participation. And above all there were the children, for whom all would be new and benign—safe places to play and fresh and decent schools.

It is amazing how quickly the suburban experience came to be sneered at, even by many of the people who were themselves taking part in it, as the rankest materialism. Having a car, a new refrigerator and freezer, and machines that would automatically wash and dry one's laundry came to be seen as the worst kind of display of that old social bugbear, keeping up with the Joneses. No end of books and articles came to be devoted to the question of why people were, to borrow the famous term of the social scientist David Riesman, so "other-directed." What is more, this indictment of the way millions upon millions of ordinary hardworking, law-abiding, middle-class Americans had chosen to live would with almost no resistance become axiomatic among all the spokesmen for American culture. Its deepest intent, whether recognized as such or not, was political: that is, as part of a time-honored continuing attack on something called "bourgeois America"—put on hold temporarily during the war and back in force.

I suppose that most of the ordinary people whose lives were being caricatured as this terrible stew of petty materialism, even if they more or less acceded to what was being said, just went on busily about their own daily affairs. That is the saving way of most ordinary people. But as everyone would learn in the not-too-distant future, the people who would turn out to be the most truly affected by the ugly characterization of suburban life would be the children meant to be its primary beneficiaries.

Happily, *Commentary,* and especially the magazine's editor in chief, Elliot Cohen, was not inclined to add its, and his, weight to any indictment of American life. On the contrary, he could sometimes wax quite sentimental about the United States, and set aside space in virtually every issue for a department called "From the American Scene" in which writers would reminisce about some typically or colorfully American experience. The magazine was certainly ideologically liberal, as were to one extent or another all its editors and contributors, particularly on such issues as civil rights. But its true animating passion was a deep hatred for Communism in any and all of its manifestations, whether the policies of and the conditions in the Soviet Union or the political and cultural behavior of European and American Communists or the liberal fellow travelers of the Communists or even the liberals whose mind-set had unknowingly been influenced by the Communists. For Communists not only murdered and oppressed wherever they ruled, and threatened American and West European security—they lied. They lied as a matter of policy and so corrupted everything within their reach. Thus that part of American life that was untainted in any way by the attitudes of Communists would, if only by implication, merit defense. Had I not in Glen Oaks received my own inoculation against the disease of despising so vast a constituency of my fellow citizens I would have certainly been given a saving shot of it there in the office of *Commentary.*

My own life in those days, however, had become far from ordinary. For one thing, though I spent a full workday in the office and then came home to spend an intense time with my two little girls before their bedtime, I was living in a state of what was to me unimaginable freedom. I was answerable to no one for my habits or my preferences. I could sit up all night or go to bed at eight o'clock with the children. I could eat a peanut butter sandwich or even just a single sardine for supper. I could sit in the bathtub for an hour and maybe even two, or, had I been of a mind to, walk barefoot in the streets. This feeling, so new, was a joy, but at the same time it was also disquieting, for when put to such a test, how was I to know what I "really" wanted to do? It sometimes seemed to me that but for those little girls, I might have gone floating off into the sky like a helium balloon.

And in those days at least, when divorce was not quite so commonplace as it was later to become, a relatively young divorcée was up against it in another way as well. I used to fancy that somewhere in the club of divorced men and no-longer-young bachelors there hangs a bulletin board on which are posted the day's new crop of divorced or widowed women. For men began to call me up: would I care to have lunch, drinks, dinner? Some of these men were old friends or acquaintances, some were casual new friends or acquaintances, some, alas, were the husbands of friends. Everyone understood what these calls were about, but they were nevertheless extremely difficult to deal with. For given the manners of the time, how could I say, sorry, I don't want to have lunch with you because I don't want to go to bed with you? On the other hand, sooner or later those lunches or drinks—dinners would naturally be out of the question—would arrive at the point where I would be required either to accede or to find a graceful way to say no without being wounding. It was far better—actually, it was a delight—just to hang out in the daytime with my playmates in the office and stick to the peanut butter and sardines at home.

Then along came my second, and last and for all times, husband, Norman Podhoretz. To remember the story of how this marriage came about still fills me, more than four decades later, with amazement and amusement. For I had actually first met him many, many years before at the seminary when he was not all that much more than a boy, and we had very quickly become friends. Good friends: I was about to be married, and he needed a female shoulder to cry on. Later he would go off to England to study, and after that into the army, so I generally lost track of him. Except for one thing: along the way, he had become a contributor to *Commentary* and had been invited to become an editor on the magazine as soon as he returned from the army. One day Bob Warshow wrote to him—he was then stationed in Germany—and said, "There is someone here who says she knows you. Her name is Midge Decter, and if her typing should ever improve, she might still be here when you arrive."

We began to correspond, and soon we were corresponding almost daily until he got back, by which time we had become good friends again; you might say, *very* good friends. And now in the *Commentary* office we would also become daily companions. As it happened, there was no rule against dating in the office. In those days, there was no need for one, because the combination of tact and discomfort usually did the trick. It did, anyway, in our case, so when I was offered another, and as it happened a better-paying, job on a relatively new and small Zionist magazine called *Midstream,* I grabbed it.

My daughters, sensing that something serious was going on with this new gentleman caller, took turns growing hot and cold toward him. If one of them was hostile, the other would be friendly. In general, they were not all that pleased with the way things were going, but he stood firm, which gave them confidence in him, while I tried as subtly as I knew how to convince them that their daddy would not consider them disloyal if they made friends with my new friend (which was a lie, and not, I am humiliated to say, the last one of its kind I ever tried to palm off on them).

So it was that a little more than a year after his return from Germany, Norman and I were married. How he lived through the doing of it I will never understand. For not surprisingly, his mother was, to understate the matter by a mile, far from pleased by the idea that her son was marrying a divorced woman with two children. At the same time, my parents were deeply suspicious of me and so managed to add their own dollop of gloom to the proceedings. We had found a big apartment into which the children and I had already moved, and the girls, though more or less reconciled to having this no longer strange man around, were nevertheless feeling skittish at the prospect of their new life. And in the meantime he was going through all kinds of painful trouble at the office: the editor in chief who had originally given him the job was still away in the hospital, and he had been left in the clutches of a colleague who was envious and resentful of him and who for the time being had been granted by default the power to make his life a misery.

Beyond all this, we were to have something like four days for a honeymoon. Anyone who believes—take the Marine Corps, for example—that difficult transitions are best gone through with as much pain as possible would have approved mightily of the conditions surrounding our getting married.

Well, live through it he did, and thereby hangs the tale of the rest of my life as a woman.

≈ 3 ≈

Having It All

NOT LONG AFTER WE WERE MARRIED, I ran smack into a problem that I suppose no longer exists to the same extent for professional women with children: and that is, the discovery that my job was costing us five dollars a week. In leaving *Commentary* and moving to that other magazine, I had raised my status to the rank of assistant editor and had increased my pay by some hardly munificent amount. But the expenses my pay was to cover had increased by a larger amount. The so-called housekeeper I had had—the mad Russian—was no longer with us, as I knew she would be much too intrusive for comfort in our new family life. Anyway she was old and tired and ready to retire.

So I commenced the seemingly endless search, nowadays familiar to millions, including even would-be appointees to a presidential cabinet, for someone who could adequately look after the children (and maybe even sweep up a little dust) while I was away at work. In general, there were only two possible ways to succeed in such a quest, neither of which was open to me. Either one could pay a great deal of money and hire a proper nanny, or import someone from a foreign country who would promise, in exchange for the cost of transportation and a commitment to help convert her visitor's visa to some kind of permanent status, to remain in one's household for the minimum of a year and a half or two. In the first case, we could not afford a proper nanny, nor did we actually want one around all the time exerting her authority. In the second place, indentured servitude was not my cup of tea. Then there were the plain illegal immigrants, mostly from Latin America, but they were not yet as plentiful as they would one day be. So we struggled for a while, first with a woman who turned out to be a drunk, then with a woman who was very loving but turned out to be crazy. (Some years later, when I went back to work, there would be, one after the other, two young girls, both just up from the South, both very pleasant to have around, and both pregnant and on welfare within the year.)

The discovery that my job was costing us money, then, came as something of a welcome relief. I could just stay home and hang out with the children and at the same time even feel that I was adding to the family coffers. Since my girls were exactly a year and five days apart, they were virtually twins, and for a long time both acted and were treated as if they were. This meant that in many ways they constituted a kind of family unit unto themselves, and it may have slightly eased the way through the rapid and upsetting changes I had imposed on their lives. Twice while we were living in Glen Oaks I had gone to work, once temporarily in a neighborhood store for the heavy weeks between Thanksgiving and Christmas and once for just four hours a day over a period of six months. Both times it had been a matter of needing some extra money while my then-husband had been between jobs; and after the divorce, of course, I had needed a job simply to live on.

And though by the time I was married again, both girls had been sent off to school for full days in a private nursery and kindergarten, now when the bus dropped them off at home, they would for a change find me waiting for them.

In time there would be two more babies—another daughter, and finally, to provide my husband with the balance never enjoyed by my father, a son. When, a few years later, these two were also tucked away in yet another theoretically benign and loving private school, I decided to go back to work again. It is true we needed some extra money to pay what were now four tuition fees, but that of course was not the only, and not a truly sufficient, reason. Sometimes I think what ultimately sent me back to work was the one most unentertaining thing about looking after children in the big city, and that was those afternoons sitting on a bench in the park while the children played. In Glen Oaks I had pretty much spent my afternoons in the same way, except for two things: the whole scene was then utterly new and very entertaining to me, and the "park" was a small patch outside my front door, and so it was a case of easy out and easy back in. In Manhattan, the outing was a production, with toys and snacks and drinks and changes of clothes (later there would be tricycles and then bicycles). Nor did I find the other mothers companionable in quite the same way: certainly none of us was of a mind to impart any confidences such as had been so freely exchanged on that front stoop, so we had no conversation except some very careful talk about the children. I remember marching into the house one late afternoon and declaring into an empty hallway, "This is my fourth child. I have put in my time on that bench!" Like most such declarations, this one could not really be acted on, and certainly not immediately, but it obviously remained hanging there in that hallway air. (Many years later, one of those little girls of mine would herself be a mommy sitting on a park bench in Manhattan, only by then she would be the *only* mommy doing so.)

The time would come when my two youngest children were slated to be in school until three in the afternoon, and I would set out yet again to find work. It would take me a couple of years of wending my way through two unsatisfactory jobs—though on a very much higher level of professional status and pay than my first two all those years ago—and at last I would find myself settled happily into being the executive editor of *Harper's*. Anyway, it takes no special insight to conclude that being at home again for those few years had left some corner of my soul in a restless condition.

I have sketched this story of working and not working precisely because I cannot believe that it is different in any significant respect from the stories that could be told by countless numbers of working mothers today. Those women who work because circumstances force them to have no difficulty recognizing the emotional and practical difficulties that their being away from home imposes on their children. But those who work, as I did, not from stark necessity but out of the need in some fashion to make their way in the world, must—at the very least for some minutes in the day and at the most for weeks or even months—suffer from the pinch of insecurity about the effect on their children of the choice they have made. Such is the inevitable price of worldly ambition. You can kid yourself about it, as I did for a while, but inevitably it comes up to bite you.

In any case, it is this difficulty in making a settlement one way or the other that is in my opinion the true Woman Problem. Not the oppression of women, to say the least a laughable proposition in the United States of America, nor the glass ceiling that so many have been relentlessly calling attention to, but rather a seemingly never-to-be-mediated internal clash of ambitions: the ambition to make oneself a noticeable place in the world and the ambition to be a good mother.

In the eye of history, these are both very recent ambitions, and they require a very special, very modern, set of conditions even to come into play. They require first of all the kind of economy and society in which young women are no longer expected to stay at home assisting their mothers but are instead expected to get an education and be employed in some way until they marry. This in turn requires the kind of energy and freedom that can only be afforded by a relatively high level of both urbanization and general prosperity. Wherever such conditions have come to obtain, they have sooner or later proven to be genuine blessings for women. In my generation, for example, it had come to be generally accepted that girls would go to college; in my children's generation, it was not so much accepted as simply assumed.

The trouble is that too many people seem to forget, or perhaps have never understood in the first place, that blessings can also be something of a burden.

Take the mechanization of housework, a boon to women's health and well-being if ever there was one. I can still remember from my early childhood what laundry day was like (and we lived better than many millions of our countrymen). We had a machine in the basement that tumbled each batch of clothes for what seemed like hours, after which they would be hand-fed through a wringer and dumped into a deep sinkful of clean water, wrung again into a second sinkful of water, then finally wrung into a clothes basket and hung outside on a clothesline to dry. Later, if the weather cooperated, they would be taken off the clothesline for ironing; but if it rained, the laundry would then have to dry somewhere indoors—quite a feat with something like ten bedsheets along with the family's clothes and maybe a tablecloth or two. Tuesday, then, would be ironing day, and everything, sheets, tablecloths, clothing, including my father's shirts, would be ironed to within an inch of its life. And so on through the week, each day its own major task—not to mention putting attractive food on the table without benefit of sophisticated kitchen gadgets or even decent refrigeration. I can still remember the excitement of our first electric refrigerator: it was called a Kelvinator and its motor was on top in a kind of beehive-shaped housing.

It was no fun, then, to keep a properly run household, but by the same token it was, and it was felt to be, a genuine achievement. Nowadays, because there is no longer any art involved, housework is sheer drudgery, to be gotten over with as quickly as possible. Unless, perhaps, one happens to be a gifted cook—and even that has been made somewhat supererogatory these days by the kinds of prepared luxury foodstuffs that are available even in some neighborhood supermarkets and take-out delicacy stores. Don't misunderstand: you would have to be crazy not to believe that the mechanization of keeping house has been an enormous boon to women. You only have to look at them, striding around the world with their healthy good looks and vitality, to know how their lives have been disburdened. But something nourishing, some inner source of pleasure and self-regard, has gone out of these lives as well.

The case of looking after one's children is an almost opposite one. Nowadays having and rearing children is an activity on which all sorts of heavy new responsibilities have been heaped. The housekeeper whose bed linen was kept white as the driven snow had been given to understand that her success as a mother would be judged by how well she also kept her children, fed them, dressed them, and taught them to behave themselves properly so that they could be accounted a credit to her. Contemporary women—among which I include my own generation as well as those that have come after—have been given a new and far more complicated set of responsibilities toward our children. The very first new kind of onus placed upon the contemporary mother—in a way, it is the one that determines all the others—is that it has largely been given to her to decide whether her baby should be allowed to exist at all. Setting aside the whole agonized issue of abortion, which in any case only intensifies the burden of decision, now that contraception is, so to speak, in her corner, it is she who must determine whether conception is to be allowed to take place: whether, in other words, it will be now, this possible baby, or later, that possible baby, or never. I think no one has yet taken the measure of just how difficult a decision this can be. Babies used to make their appearance in a woman's life whether they had been willed by her to do so or not, and thus their arrival tended to be much more an act of nature to be submitted to, like the rainfall. So her relation to them was that of simple submission. But for her to be given a new kind of power over life or death means that everything about this baby, its health, its beauty, its temperament, its intelligence, will somehow turn out to be either to her credit or to her demerit.

The power granted her by birth control has naturally resulted in an even greater boon to her health and vitality than being relieved of household drudgery; nowadays it even affords her the likelihood that she will live to be an energetic and attractive old lady. But as I said, it has also perforce placed her in a frequently anxiety-driven relation to motherhood. A modern mother is someone whose success is measured not by her children's civilized behavior (though that, too, of course) but by the palpable evidence in their behavior of her loving and imaginative attention to them. Such evidence would consist of their being temperamentally relaxed and unfearful, say, or of their giving signs of an eager and cheerful responsiveness to the world around them and an unambivalent affection for the people close to them. The shortcut way of saying this is that they are supposed to be a tribute to her talent as a mother. They have, in other words, become a kind of career. But since like all other human beings children cannot manage to be truly, energetically happy for more than half an hour at a time—and unlike adults cannot yet dissemble—the ambitious mother must, to borrow from T. S. Eliot, measure out her success in coffee spoons.

So it is that nowadays a young American woman of even modest means has energy to burn (which is why she can so often be seen doing such things as running for miles to no place in particular or practicing dance aerobics or working out in gymnasiums), and can at the same time find herself emotionally enervated by the end of her day.

All of this was to be somewhat alleviated in my case and that of my contemporaries by the way that many if not most of us, ourselves children of generally scanty households, were hell-bent on making good-sized families. For the more small people you have around, in your own house and the houses of all the people around you, the more likely you are to lighten up at least a little about what must be achieved. But in the end, even for us there could be only so much good humor about parenthood, for whether we had acceded to doing so or not, we were all then living in the shadow of Sigmund Freud—and the shadow of Sigmund Freud is a place of both high attentiveness and little relaxation.

Decades later, many people who took a dim view of the baby boom generation accounted for the children's generally unruly behavior by referring to the influence on their upbringing of Dr. Benjamin Spock. Dr. Spock's book, *Baby and Child Care,* had indeed been the most widely used pediatric home reference work among my cohort of young mothers, and as ignorant as we were, we had sometimes clung to that book as to a lifesaver. But poor old Dr. Spock was afterward given a bum rap, for his general message to us had been no more than to relax, that if the baby had shown this sign or that of having trouble, chances are it was nothing serious, nor did a baby need to be toilet trained by one year, and so on. No, it was Freud—often caricatured and perverted, often ignored in everything but his mode of therapy—whose influence hovered over us and put the chill of too much consciousness in our child rearing.

Hamlet said that "conscience doth make cowards of us all," and when it came to us, especially to us women, as parents, truer words were never spoken. It was not necessary for anyone to know the intellectual source of the overattention we paid to our children's emotional states and the kind of tiptoeing around that was all too frequently our response to them. These things had been written into the culture, first into the high culture by the intellectual devotees of Freudianism, and from there, as usual, into the general ethos where they came to dictate the norms for all decent people. Freud himself had unquestionably had something else in mind than the spectacle of the gaucheries of certain of our child-rearing practices. He had very different fish to fry from the mothering programs of modern young American women. Nevertheless, by his ripest fruits shall ye know him.

Another burden that the great old doctor, or rather certain of his venturesome followers, placed upon us (and that we in turn wittingly or unwittingly placed upon our children) was a preoccupation with something called "good sex." Good sex basically meant the participation of women in the full range of the pleasures of sexual intercourse, including—or in the view of certain famous experts, especially—orgasm. To begin with, the idea of good sex was born in the early-twentieth-century rebellion against what was almost universally understood to be the repression and priggishness of the Victorian age, and must at the time have seemed to be the height of subversion of the established order. (It has sometimes occurred to me to wonder how the idea of sexual repression could have been so confidently associated with the name of a woman as utterly besotted with her husband as Queen Victoria.)

Whatever its origin, in the end the quest for the female orgasm meant that where once a woman in bed was supposed to be pliant and helpful, now she was supposed to be demanding. Where once sexual relations followed from a surrender to the urgency of the man's need and desire, now sex would not be a surrender but an effort, at the end of which both man and woman would be accounted either a success or a failure. All this was supposed to represent a long-needed evening of the score between the sexes, but there were two deeply questionable assumptions behind it: first, that there could be no sexual pleasure or fulfillment for women without orgasm, and second, that in achieving it (and "achieving" was certainly the word by the time the experts were finished with her) she would be made whole, a fulfilled and contented woman.

And if being a mother inevitably led her to a new set of concerns about success and failure, what can one say about sex? Each time she failed to have an orgasm, she would be invited by all current theory to account her failure to some shortcoming in herself as a woman (despite the fact that her husband or lover would now be required to place the blame on himself as well). So whatever else this new sexual dispensation might have been in the life of one or another individual woman, it was hardly calculated to sweeten relations between the sexes. And for many of the ordinary young couples of my day, concerned with such stresses as making an adequate living and doing right by the children, it proved far more of a burden than a life enhancement.

(How it would have amazed us to know that only four decades or so into the future all of the women's magazines, whether devoted to fashion or health, would feature instruction in almost every issue about how to enhance sexual pleasure—not their own, but *their men's*. "Ten Ways to Drive Him Wild in Bed" would be a typical cover line meant to entice the women in the checkout line.)

Anyway, all this is not to suggest that the young postwar families I am talking about did not have an easier life all around than their counterparts in the past. Rarely did their infants sicken and die, for instance, a blow that used to land on people in olden times with what would be to us a literally unimaginable frequency. Rarely did a young husband die of a dread disease or a young wife die in childbirth. And rarely did anyone grow old and bent before his time from such things as the combination of brutal physical work and poor nutrition. But if they were better off than people like them had ever been before, here or anywhere in the world, they did suffer from one entirely new and unprecedented deprivation: they could no longer simply take for granted what it was that life asked or expected of them.

As for me, not only did I not know what life expected of me, I would not for some years figure out what I wanted from it, either. This is what my grandmother would have called a *goldene tsoreh,* a golden trouble. I wanted to work, that was clear: as seldom as I dared admit it to myself, like all small-town girls who dream of coming to New York, I was smitten with the dream of making something of myself. But I also wanted my children to have a good time of it. This was a conflict I never resolved as the years passed: I would be in the world of work and out again and then in again. It would take a very long time for me to understand that I needn't have gone through these shenanigans, that I could have gone to work when the youngest of my children was in high school, or maybe even off to college. But just as the young never really understand, or believe, that there is a long, long time stretching ahead of them in which to do all the things they want, so many young mothers like me have felt—and no doubt continue to feel—that if they don't move on the question of career now, the world will simply pass them by.

So I wangled myself a job and cheered myself up with the idea that my children were getting along okay and that we truly needed the money on account of all that tuition we were paying. And my cheer only increased after some undeserved stroke of luck brought into my life a young, kind, gentle, intelligent woman from Belize named Imelda. I could not pay her what she was actually worth "on the market," though being an illegal immigrant, and timid, she had no idea what she was worth. I tried to make up for the shortfall of money and to keep her with us by seeing to it that she first became a legal immigrant and then a citizen and then got herself a high-school equivalency degree. Meanwhile, the children claimed her for their own. She played with them, scolded them, fed them, kept track of one of my daughters' favorite soap operas so she could relay the day's developments when the child returned home from school, and in general hung close to the youngest, my son. So that part of the problem seemed to me to be as well taken care of as I dared to hope.

I would then pass through two jobs before I could feel that I had landed where I wanted to be. The first was interesting but required a dreadfully long and inconvenient trip away from home. I had persuaded Herman Kahn, the man who famously dared to think through the possibilities of nuclear war and for his pains became the putative model for Dr. Strangelove, to take me on as an editor. That people could imagine this large, fat, kind, cheerful, brilliant, and far-seeing man as some kind of evil madman taught me an early lesson—of many such lessons to come—about the potential for sheer ugliness in ideological politics. Herman had put together a think tank devoted mainly to defense and foreign policy issues, which was located in an exurb a goodly distance up the Hudson River from New York City. I would land there each day after a trip by subway, train, and bus and feel totally out of touch with home, and after a few months I gave up. The second job was to work at CBS Records, in what was basically a kind of vanity press put together at the behest, and for the pleasure, of the company's president, Goddard Lieberson. We published books that were meant to be packaged with records. This was an impossible job, not because of Lieberson, who was charming, but because there was not a single member of our little enterprise who had the faintest idea about what he was doing or how to do it. It was strictly amateur night in Dixie. Fortunately, I was soon to be rescued.

Now, women who go to work full-time in an office learn something about the world that women who stay home may not fully understand or appreciate—and that is, what it means to have a boss: someone who determines what it is you are to do each day and who has at least as great a power as your mate, and maybe greater, to make your daily life pleasant or unpleasant, as the case may be. And whether he does one or the other—again, as people who do not work at jobs may not understand—depends not on the sweetness of his demeanor but on his competence. It is generally true that being competent and decisive tends to keep a person in good humor, but even should he (or she) not be especially pleasant, the general feeling that things are under control and proceeding as they should be is what makes an office a cheerful place. Obversely, having to work under the supervision of a kind and sympathetic superior who is at the same time incapable of doing what is necessary for furthering the common enterprise is sooner or later bound to breed anxiety all the way down the line. Having had so many jobs in my life, ranging all the way from the most primitively clerical to a fairly high level of skill and responsibility, I have naturally had all kinds of bosses (and have even been one myself). I have generally been extremely lucky, but two of these bosses stand out for having given me and everyone else in the office a very bad time. They were very different, these two men, one who believed that the way to retain his power was by doing nothing but playing the sycophant to the man at the top of the totem pole, and the other, who was at the top of his own pole but who could not make up his mind what he really wanted to do there. Both were nice as pie—and to be escaped from at the earliest possibility.

This was an important lesson to learn about the working life. If I were teaching in a school of business, I would design a course called "The Boss 101." It does seem to me, though, that the nature of bosses is an easier problem for a woman to manage than it is for a man, perhaps because women are somehow better manipulators of their surroundings, nor is their amour propre so immediately or so painfully engaged as it is in men.

But still, for the working mother—particularly if she is still young—there is worry enough to be getting on with.

Eventually I landed at *Harper's* magazine, where I was to have a wonderful time, surrounded by colleagues I liked and respected and with whom I would drink many a beer and share many a laugh. More than that, under the editorship of Willie Morris, a Mississippi boy bred on the love of serious literature, *Harper's* had virtually overnight been turned into a writers' magazine and was in the process of becoming what is called in the trade a "hot book." This added immeasurably to the fun. I was soon given the title of executive editor, which meant that in addition to the ordinary editorial duties—basically shared among three of us—I was put in charge of the housekeeping connected with getting the magazine onto the press. But in publishing especially, perhaps because the pay is hardly glamorous, a title maketh the man—or, of course, the woman.

And thereby hangs an instructive tale. Many of those young women at Yale to whom I would later administer such a shock, along with countless others like them in places like Harvard, Bryn Mawr, Vassar, et al., do make their way into publishing, often doing jobs for which being a secretary would, but for the

horror of the title, be a great step up. At *Harper's* there had
been a few of these young women, mostly hanging around
with not too much to do, reading the slush pile and writing
silly critical comments on manuscripts that would then be cir-
culated. I'm afraid I put a stop to that, and to them, the day I
found on my desk the manuscript of a poem by the eminent
poet John Berryman to which was affixed a reader's note saying, "This poet is too dull and derivative. Reject." I hit the
ceiling, and one by one the slush-pile ladies left us. There were,
however, two real secretaries in the office, one of them a sullen
beauty who was clearly in a state of longing for some indeter-
minate change in her life, and one who was a full-blown flower
child planning one day to take her "old man" and her loom
and move to Nova Scotia. These two girls stood out from the
rest by being actually perfectly competent at their jobs. And I
could only shake my head at what was to become of them.
This was the late sixties. Young women, particularly young
women from the best schools, had begun to express great anger
with their lot in life; and one day, the two of them marched
into Willie Morris's office to lay before him their demand,
which was not for more pay but for new titles. Willie, I think,
was quite bewildered and said, of course, if it meant so much to
them, why not? Well, now that she was an editorial assistant,
the beauteous one began to find it harder and harder to get to
work on time, and increasingly often, to get to work at all. The
other, our flower child, just grew angrier and angrier. They
had been so intent on raising what sociologists call their ascrip-
tive status that they had not stopped to ask themselves just how
these new titles were supposed to be affecting their lives or
their work. In the event, of course, they hadn't changed anything, except, in one case, to undermine whatever small
amount of conscientiousness the newly dubbed editorial assis-

tant had ever felt toward her job. Willie and they had both been wrong in imagining that this merely titular improvement in their standing would be the answer to their inner demand. It seems that no one in charge of their instruction along the way had ever told them that the way to ascend in the world was to accept greater, not lesser, responsibility. And because Willie himself was so deceptively relaxed in manner, he would have been the last person to help them understand that his status and title as editor in chief was entirely proportional to the burden he had agreed to carry.

In the end, Willie would make another error of judgment, though of a very different kind and far more serious, with respect to the power of status. A business manager had been imposed upon him by the magazine's owner, and there came the day when the two were at daggers drawn over some question of policy. That Willie was in the right in this dispute was not by itself enough for him to do what he did: namely, lay his job on the line. He had not properly taken the measure of the owner, who was in many ways a foolish man, and in no way more foolish than his totally impossible ambition for the magazine to be profitable; and he had not taken the measure of the business manager, who, when the dust settled, was the one left standing.

After what literary gossip held to be a very dramatic (and was in fact a foolish and unnecessary) confrontation with his boss, Willie walked out, claiming that his editorial freedom had been interfered with. The press then took up his cry, relishing the spectacle of what Willie had termed "the men of literature against the men of money." After which the rest of the editorial staff were then required to walk out with him, ostensibly in loyalty to the "men of literature," or suffer a serious impairment of reputation. Only one stayed on, a writer named Lewis Lapham, who had only a short time before been named a "contributing editor" against the wishes of everyone else on the editorial staff and had as yet done virtually nothing for the magazine. Is it necessary to mention that in only a few short years the erstwhile contributing editor became, and has ever since remained, the editor in chief?

I was mad at Willie for not working harder to protect his enterprise, and burning with resentment at *Time* and *Newsweek,* who loved to turn everything into the same cheap drama of good editors and bad old businessmen and thereby forced us all to quit or have our names blackened. So back home I went, wondering what would happen next.

After a bump or two, and a hiatus for the purpose of being at home with my youngest, my future working life would in many respects, especially the money, be better. But it would never again be so unexpectedly sweet.

And now it is time for me to introduce my children. By the time I walked out of *Harper's* my oldest, Rachel, was twenty years old, and my youngest, my son John, ten. I have not spoken much about them as individuals until now, partly to protect their privacy—there is nothing so irritating as to find oneself appearing in a book where the author, even if she is your mother, does not quite see things as you did, or leaves out what you know to be decisive details—and partly to protect myself from having to confess the sins I have committed against them. Anyone who saw the four of them today, three daughters and one son, would never credit that Rachel and Naomi, the two oldest, are only half siblings of Ruth and John, the two youngest. For not only is there not a drop of alienation or distance between any two of them, each is thoroughly entangled in the lives of the others and they have only now and then, at least as adults, even been consequentially angry with one another. I have no idea how this happened, nor does my husband; having both of us been children who one way and another were given to feeling some amount of alienation from our respective families, we have watched this four-way relationship developing under our noses with a certain degree of puzzlement and a great deal of pleasure-filled wonderment. Nor has either of us found any way to take even the least bit of credit for it: some blessings, like some sorrows, are handed out we-know-not-why.

Nor could they be more dissimilar in temperament or personality. The two oldest, being almost exactly a year apart, have grown into their forties almost like twins, though there could hardly be two women more unlike: one with the demeanor of a perpetual enthusiast behind which is concealed a mind, and wit, of pure steel; the other all apparently steady and practical and clever with the soul of a romantic. (The deeper truth about them has made its way to the surface in their respective first-born sons, the elder wickedly clever and the younger a true poet.) Number three daughter, a divorcée who lives with her four children in Jerusalem, when she was young used to keep us all amused (except for her younger brother), and now as a grown-up woman is blessed with a vast amount of a quality that is best characterized as mother-wit. And there is my son, who is the baby of the family and who both benefited and suffered from having been preceded and surrounded by three rather colorful big sisters. He is the one who also paid the highest price for my career, having been the one most uninterruptedly left to the care of others. And he has been gifted—or perhaps the word is laden—with such a variety of literary interests and talents it has always been hard to know where, or how, he will ever get to make use of all of them. This can best be illustrated by the most vivid picture we all have of him from his childhood, which is of this little boy, maybe eight years old, lying on the floor watching television with one foot in the air and spread before him bits of paper on which he is composing a play whose hero might be Charlie Chaplin. He was everybody's (again, with the exception of his next-older sister) darling, perpetually amusing, and we put impossible pressure on him.

I certainly can't claim for myself that I was a good mother—indeed, I sometimes wonder if anyone really can—but one crime I did not commit against my children: I did not and do not now fail to know who they are.

≈ 4 ≈

Memories of the
Words of Women

ONE DAY WHILE I WAS WORKING at *Harper's* I was invited to
have lunch with a woman with whom I was on pleasant terms
but did not really know all that well. She and her husband happened to be friendly with close friends of ours, and we would
meet now and then at dinner. Her husband was a successful
lawyer and she was a high-muck-a-muck in a big publishing
house. We chatted about this and that. She told me about a
book she was bringing out for which she had great hopes. The
author of the book was a teacher of philosophy and, said my
acquaintance, she had overnight become a guru to young
women, who were rushing in droves to hear her lectures. I
nodded politely; publishers at lunch always had a book that
they talked about in that way. Then suddenly, as it were out of
nowhere, she leaned over the table with a look of unhappy intensity and asked me, "Does your husband ever talk to you

about his work when he gets home at night?" I was completely taken aback, and about to laugh—does he ever shut up about it would have been a more appropriate question—but I could see that she was in no mood for laughter. So I sputtered something about the mystery of husbands, and left it at that. She, however, wanted to go further into the subject, though why with me in particular I did not know, and to this day cannot imagine. It seemed that her husband didn't like to talk about his lawyering when he got home at night, and she felt patronized by this.

How was I to respond? That maybe like many other lawyers I knew he was bored to death with his work and was looking for a change of subject when he got home? If true, I suppose he could have told her that himself. I had listened to the sad tales of women with husband problems many times over the years, but this one was something new.

To my relief, or so I thought, we then switched back to talk about publishing. Now, this woman happened to be sitting on what the overwhelming majority of working women in the world would have considered the top of the heap; the next stop would have put her among the corporate bosses (and in a few years, that's just about where she would end up, though in another publishing house). But it turned out that as with her husband, she also had a basketful of grievances against her male colleagues. It seems they insisted on continuing to regard her as, in her words, "merely a woman," because from time to time manuscripts would be forwarded to her from other divisions of the company with the request that she provide the woman's point of view on whether or not they might sell.

I almost literally staggered away from that lunch. What was going on here that an attractive, successful, well-heeled, and in all ways enviable woman should be suddenly so laden down with complaint? When I told my husband of this lunch conversation, his response was something that many times in the future would serve as a kind of tag line covering our observations of marital difficulty: "What does her husband say to her when he gets home? 'Don't bother your pretty little head about torts'?"

A few years earlier, I had read a huge best-seller called *The Feminine Mystique* written by a to-me unknown woman named Betty Friedan, but as I confessed earlier, I had simply failed to take the book's, and her, measure as a phenomenon. The work had seemed to me both intellectually and stylistically very crude. It was also unbelievably insulting to ordinary housewives, written on the level and in exactly the kind of lingo previously used by a number of pop sociologists to denigrate the postwar lives of the ordinary people of Glen Oaks.

The housewives in *The Feminine Mystique* appeared to be living far better than had my old Glen Oaks neighbors: they had, for instance, become far more affluent and had found themselves much better places in which to live. But, Betty Friedan was trying to tell us, they were suffering from a malaise so dreadful and so deep-going that it had no name. Their lives were empty and so, as a consequence, were their minds and spirits, many of them, in Betty Friedan's opinion, being akin to those veterans who had returned home from the war with brain damage. What? I had asked myself. My old buddy the ever-lively Leila—who was so powerful she commanded a whole gang of neighbors, who was so keen on moving to a house that every week she read the real estate sections of three newspapers, who had the hots for Clark Gable, who spent the summer of her second pregnancy tanning her legs so that they would look attractive on the delivery table—now dull and empty? Not bloody likely.

Still, Betty Friedan said that she had spoken with many

groups of suburban women at specially organized kaf-
feeklatsches, and under her guidance they had haltingly but
with growing relief begun to speak to her of their sorrows. It
seems that what had really happened to them is that they had
been dumped into these lonely communities, in which from
sunup to sundown there was not a man to be seen, and left
there to spend empty days enslaved to the needs of their children. Their absent men meanwhile were naturally off in the
big city, whooping it up day after day and often at night as well,
leaving them to grow ever more hopeless and depressed.

I could understand some woman's feeling that she had made a
mistake in wanting to live in the suburbs: had I myself not run
back into town at the first opportunity? But I happened to
know a lot of women who remained there; they were friends,
colleagues, relatives, and they didn't seem either oppressed or
depressed to me. Some went back to work when their children
were old enough, some became active in local civic organizations, some got interested in politics and worked their hearts out
for this or that candidate or ballot measure, some kept up a running fight about some problem or other in the local schools,
one remained a convinced and unreconstructed slattern, and
one in particular became a mad lifelong gardener. And finally,
many of my contemporaries had moved away from town on account of the educational degradation of the city schools—in
short, to offer a better opportunity to their kids. Sometimes
they were deceived in this, the reputation of suburban schools
often being ridiculously overblown (but then, those of us who
attempted to deal with the issue of our children's education
through private schools in the city were also sometimes deceived). The point is, living in the suburbs was the result of a
decision rather than the imposition of either an unjust God or a
sexist society. Those who made that decision, being free Ameri-

can people, male or female, could have unmade it. There was something very unpleasant to me about the idea that in a world which had only recently witnessed so much suffering and death—women not consigned to a dull life, for example, but being burnt to ashes—one should be asked to extend some special sympathy to women who were hands down among the luckiest, healthiest, and freest people on earth. Be that as it may, I had not yet really grasped what Mrs. Friedan represented, thinking of her book as merely another in the series of generally left-inspired attacks on the nature of American society.

After the immediate and enormous success of *The Feminine Mystique,* and no doubt in the glow of that success, Betty Friedan next put together an organization called the National Organization for Women (NOW). This, it will be remembered, was a time for new movements and organizations. Martin Luther King and the young civil rights activists in the South had by the combination of the justice of their cause and the sheer dauntlessness and nobility of their methods stirred the juices of activism in many a northerner who now wanted for himself a taste of how it would feel to change the world. Groups of northern students began to picket Woolworth's five-and-dimes with as much fervor as if it were they rather than black kids in the South who had been denied service at their lunch counter. And so it was, too, that NOW, which never from then until now succeeded in signing up as many as three hundred thousand women[1] would be granted the title of "the women's movement." The southern civil rights groups

---

1. For purposes of comparison, Hadassah, an organization of American Zionist women—that is, an organization of a particular ideological segment of a community that itself constituted only about 2 or 2½ percent of the American population—had a membership of something like 350,000.

happened to be battling real villains in the persons of Jim Crow officials and the citizens who had without protest agreed to be governed by these officials. The villains in the case of the women's movement were—who else in all logic could they be?—men. All categories of men: husbands, bosses, professors, officials, politicians, and fathers. (Amazingly, Betty Friedan would later disclaim any connection between what she had been saying and hostility to men.)

But even the existence of NOW might not have seemed so notable a development to me. The oppression business was booming, and the ones that to begin with I was paying the most attention to were the so-called radical students. They were the children of all those postwar families who had been so intent on bringing them into the world and giving them good lives. They were nearly adults, these students, and they were behaving more out of control than I had ever seen them do on a bad day in the sandpile. They were blockading buildings, setting fires in libraries, throwing rocks, defecating in university buildings, fighting with the police. Some were merely getting zonked on drugs, and some were dropping out of school and running off to some faraway countryside to "make their lives anew," at times in a cloud of drugs. What had started out as activities like picketing Woolworth's, undertaken in order to stir in themselves some imitation of the bravery of those black kids in the South, had in only a few short years turned merely ugly. The people who were determined to excuse these so-called rebels, including, of course, many of their own parents, said they were protesting against the war in Vietnam. But that seemed to me just a convenient excuse. Had they actually been trying to influence American policy, they would: one, not have picked on their universities, most of whose faculties and administrations were in complete agreement about the war, and two, have joined together with all the adults who shared their opinion on the war in a serious show of respectable political force that might have had some impact on Washington. Nothing could have been further from what I think they were really up to, which was to express their rebellion against the expectation that they would one day have to take their places in the ongoing flow of life. All one had to do was *listen* to them—I mean the music, not the words—to see that ending the war would be simple compared to what they were after.

This came home to me most vividly when, one day at the time of the Great Columbia University Protest, I witnessed a scene that has never left my mind. In those days we were living not far from the Columbia campus, which happens to be just across the street from its sister all-girls college, Barnard, and we used to walk by there fairly often. Well, on the afternoon I am talking about here was the scene: on one side of the street was the Columbia campus, now closed off to the outside by some kind of barrier. Behind the barrier stood a crowd of students who were screaming imprecations at a group of young cops walking back and forth on the other side of the barrier looking as if they weren't sure what they were supposed to be doing. And just across the street, hanging out of the windows of their dormitory, were several Barnard girls shouting obscenities and waving their brassieres and panties. I saw one of the cops look up at what was going on across the street, and on his face was an unforgettable look, a look made up in equal parts of shock, rage, and longing. These were the kind of affluent, private-college girls that this young cop would have been far too socially intimidated to get mixed up with, and yet here they were, with mouths like street bums', making obscene gestures at him. The look on that boy's face by itself taught me something about the 1960s that few people then or since have ever thought to mention, namely, that the student riots and the cops' response to them were not merely a case of rebellious kids against the might of the Authorities, even though they were virtually everywhere in this society being represented as such. On the contrary: what I was witnessing was a war of the privileged young against the working-class young. Those cops were also "kids" (as were the boys who went to Vietnam instead of contriving to get themselves exempted). The great revolution of the sixties and seventies, in other words, turned out to be little more than a class war in which the affluent had the better weapons: the indulgence of parents and teachers along with virtually the whole of the press and the clergy.

This was what I saw that day as I was walking outside of Columbia and Barnard. Many of my friends in the literary and publishing world did not see it that way. After what they considered the too-responsible life in the fifties, they were only too happy to sign on to the supposed revolution and in that way enjoy a belated touch of the restlessness of youth. They came to think me shockingly mean-spirited when I spoke of the folk my husband and I began referring to as "the youngs," and I came to think them far too careless about the welfare of those who were after all our children, and so we quarreled—until all too quickly we had reached the point of no return.

In my own household, my two elder daughters, thanks in very large part to my doughty husband who had no compunction about expressing his profound opposition to what was going on, managed to stay just this side of the culture of the revolution. The younger of the two teenagers in any case seemed to have been born with what Ernest Hemingway once referred to as a "built-in shit detector" and had very little to do with the cultural forces all around her. Moreover, any tendency she might have had to weaken in the face of peer pressure was completely put to rest on the day when, as her classmates were making plans to hold some kind of demonstration against the Vietnam War in front of their school, one of the boys announced that as his contribution to the demonstration he would set his dog on fire.

Her older sister, however, who would not until much later in life own up to having her own equipment for sniffing out fakery, marched alongside her contemporaries and, when no one was looking, saved herself from the worst of the calamities—mainly brought about by drugs—that were overtaking them. A number of her friends, alas, were not so wise (or so lucky as to have had my absolutely unintimidated husband acting as their father—their own having generally absconded some time before).

Meanwhile, it would turn out that many of the coeds in the radical student movement were growing restless and resentful. They were, they claimed, being consigned to an inferior position by their brutish male comrades. The movement men may have pretended that they were out to overturn the world, said their female comrades, but they were still taking unto themselves the exclusive right to make policy while the girls were expected to do all the scut work, making coffee, running errands, and typing. Furthermore, they were offended to the point of no return when at a big conference of radicals their putative black "brother" Stokely Carmichael declared that the proper posture for women in the revolution was on their backs. This was the last straw; they stormed out of the conference and declared that from now on they would be making a revolution of their own.

And as it would turn out, theirs would be a revolution to put storming campus buildings and spilling pigs' blood in Selective Service files completely to shame.

After having at first foolishly failed to give NOW my full attention, I now read *The Feminine Mystique* again, this time more closely, and even though I continued to find it crude in its social analysis and deeply insulting to women, it was no longer mysterious to me that the book should have become a huge best-seller. For the truth was, books attacking any aspect of the lives of middle-class Americans in those days usually sold extremely well—to middle-class Americans, and to the women among them particularly. We were a generation uniquely prone to gobbling up all cultural artifacts devoted to detailing our weaknesses. In the case of the Friedan book in particular, I could see the seductiveness for a certain kind of woman in the idea that the way her life turned out had nothing to do with her, that she had come to spend her days in a peculiar state of restlessness because she had all along been a victim of oppression. But in all the public appearances surrounding her book Betty Friedan herself was so shrill and lacking in gravitas it was still hard for me to imagine that anyone could seriously take up the standard and march behind her.

And then there was the surprising case of Gloria Steinem. I had known Gloria in her previous life as a very beautiful, very sexy, friendly and pleasant young journalist around town with a so-so talent and a decent if not distinguished career. One day it was announced to me by a common acquaintance that she had become something of a spokesman for this new feminist movement that seemed to be springing up everywhere. Soon after I heard about what happened to Gloria I was asked if I would agree to debate her by some union friends of mine who were trying to convince the AFL–CIO leaders (in vain, as it would turn out) that it would be a violation of the sacred union principle of seniority to create a new system of special considera-

tion for women. To my surprise Gloria had agreed to participate in such a debate, so I agreed as well.

The debate took place in a downtown ballroom that often
served as a union meeting place, and the room was packed. Actually there were four women debating that night, on her side a
black social worker and on mine, a black official of the teachers' union. Gloria was unforgettable that evening, for she
turned up in a crotch-high suede skirt and knee-high suede
boots and kept warning the men in the audience that they had
better wake up and realize that she and women like her were
dead serious, and no longer were women going to put up with
being their playthings. I think she even stamped her foot, while
I, looking at that skirt, had to control my impulse to giggle:
how to issue men a stern warning to back off while affording
them a juicy glimpse of thigh. Where I grew up, we used to
call that "teasing." Later in the evening she declared that
women no longer needed men and that men had better get
used to it, whereupon her own debating partner jumped up
and said, "*Oh no,* Gloria! What the women in *Harlem* need is
husbands!"

Not long after that a very expensively and glamorously
turned out young woman came to the office—she may have
wanted to write something for us, I can't exactly remember—
who told me that she was one of those disciples of the feminist
philosopher I had heard about at lunch, and that she traveled to
anywhere in the country where the woman was lecturing. She
spoke of her eyes having been opened to the raw deal that
civilization had for millennia been giving women and of the
exciting freedom that had come with her new level of compre-
hension. She was now her own woman, she declared, dependent on no one, especially on no man. Whereupon she got up,

walked uninvited into Willie's office, sat down by his desk waiting for him to finish a phone conversation, lifted her skirt—as
Gloria Steinem had done—high on the thigh, and invited him
out to lunch. Willie, who always used the "I'm-just-a-poor-
country-boy-from-Mississippi" act to get himself out of a tight
spot, managed to hold her off by marching her back to me and
making a quick getaway.

Much of this new women's movement and its putative rage
against men therefore seemed to me at first to have more to do
with show business than with social revolution. The trouble
was, the subject kept making me laugh. And looking back, I
would say that it took two things, a couple of years apart, to
make me really understand that we were in the presence of
something truly radical. The first, of course—because despite
my husband's wisecracking, I continued to be puzzled over it—
was my lunch with that successful woman publisher with the
seemingly unsharing husband. For by the time of our lunch I
had been visited by scores of privileged young women out of
college who were looking for a job "in publishing" and who
would have sold their bodies, their souls, and their grandmothers to find themselves in her position. What, then, was really
going on with my lunch companion? Was she afraid to be a
boss—I heard later from a couple of people who worked for
her that she was a particularly bad one—and, like those secretaries at *Harper's,* was turning sour with her new responsibilities
and looking to blame the world? Or had she really been convinced that someone's seeking advice from her "as a woman"
was a profound insult? In either case, she was taking an enviable
life and turning it bitter. That was a serious matter to contemplate.

And then there began to cross my desk a series of pamphlets
and articles and collections of essays in book form that were

neither laughable nor curious but just plain frightening. They were so full of violence and loathing—against men and women and sex and babies—there was no longer the possibility of mistaking both the true radicalism and the very real danger of this particular liberation movement. I set out to read every word of every one of these books and collections of essays, and it soon occurred to me that no one else, including the editors of the publishing houses that had published them, had dared to pay even the slightest attention to what they were actually saying. Which was, that for thousands of years women had been kept down and exploited by men who had once glimpsed, and been terrified by, their power. This exploitation, they said, took every possible form: enslavement to men's sexual desires, enslavement to the need for keeping the home fires burning, enslavement to the race by virtue of their having wombs, and, in modern industrial societies, the enslavement of poor women to the lowest forms of work and pay and of affluent women to the empty boredom of being no more than symbols of their husbands' success. If this were not enough, there was the special exploitation of women arising from the quest for their own sexual pleasure, which required them to do such demeaning things as pretending to feel the same erotic desire as their mates and counterfeiting orgasm.

And this little summary says nothing about the manner in which many of the charges were leveled, to wit, unspeakably crude and dirty-mouthed. And as for me, I was now, at long last, listening, truly listening, to the women who came to be known as Libbers, and I did not always find it easy to decide just where their hatred was truly being directed, at men or really at women. They most certainly said horrible things about themselves, beginning with the idea—whose logic seemed to escape them—that everything women had been given by nature to do was by definition unjust and inferior. But then there was no reasoning involved in all this; it was just a large and long-lasting explosion.

One of the contributors to an early Lib publication[2] wrote that a woman she had been reading about had within the space of one brief period encountered nine impotent men. "What better revenge," she joyously commented, "can a much-victimized woman perpetrate than to wilt the pricks of nine randy men? It might be a baseball team—or the whole Supreme Court!"

A different but related kind of comment appeared in the most famous and successful of the anthologies, *Sisterhood Is Powerful* (published in 1970 and still available in the women's studies sections of bookstores). Here a woman complains that after working at a dull job all day and coming home to fix dinner, she stands at the sink to do the dishes when her husband begins to make sexual advances to her. "He naively expects," she comments, "that these advances will fill her with passion, melting all anger, and result not only in her forgetting and forgiving but in gratitude and renewed love. . . . A couple of screws and the slate is wiped clean. Who needs to pay for servants or buy his wife a washing machine when he has a cock?"[3]

These passages were by no means out of the ordinary for this literature, and there were many others even more foul-mouthed, written by various self-identified lesbians for whom Women's Liberation has, naturally, been a walk in the park. Anyway, lesbian or "straight," the undeniable import of the movement's literary outpouring was that men, all men—

2. Leah Fritz, "Bitchpower," *New York Element,* November–December 1971.
3. Beverly Jones, "The Dynamics of Marriage and Motherhood," *Sisterhood Is Powerful,* 1970.

husbands, fathers, lovers, bosses—were oppressive louts, if not worse. (Some of the mothers in the movement even decided that they had to emasculate their little sons by bringing them up gender-free.)

And the husbands, fathers, lovers, bosses? For the most part, they commenced simply to walk on eggs with females, pretending not to notice what the women's movement was saying about them, and saved any expression of self-defense or resentment for their locker-room conversations.

Why men should have responded with so much timidity in the face of so violent an assault on them I could not understand then and, truth to tell, I do not understand it to this day. Many explanations have been given to me by one or another of them, usually having to do with sex and the guilt toward women for failures therein, but these sound too glib to be true. A man might feel apologetic toward one woman, or maybe even toward several, for sexual shortcomings—but toward the *whole of womankind,* especially when a number of them are screaming imprecations at him? Something else had to have been going on.

One afternoon back in the height of all this female violence and male avoidance, my husband and I were out walking with our eldest daughter, who happened to be an especially pretty girl in her early twenties, when we ran into an old acquaintance. He was someone we had not seen in quite a while, so we stopped to talk. As we were saying good-bye, he pulled me aside and said, "I would tell your daughter that she is a very attractive young woman but I am afraid I would offend her." So quickly and so far had the movement worked its effect. This man happened to be someone with a loving wife and children who was in turn a loving husband and father, and yet even he was walking around on tiptoe. I assured him she would be very far from offended, but from that day to this I have not been able to get over his craven sappiness.

In only a few short years all this stuff would enter the universities, whose authorities had, as a response to student violence, gone heavily into placating people with angry demands. Women's studies courses were with no resistance accredited and, like black studies courses, permitted the status of leading to a degree.

My old friend Bayard Rustin, an eminent black civil rights leader, had virtually torn his hair out over black studies: "We fought and fought, people suffered, to get black kids into universities so that they could have new opportunities," he used to lament, "and now these university administrations are allowing them to go all through school studying their oppression and playing bongo drums." What, then, could one say about the young women whose rights to higher education, insofar as they had to be fought for at all, had been secured four generations earlier and who were giving up the possibility of getting themselves rigorously trained for serious careers in order to wallow in the history of their own putative oppression? For such after all was the underlying purpose of women's studies, included among whose tutelary misdemeanors has been the touting of many a mediocre to downright third-rate literary work that had the good fortune to have been written by a woman. At the same time some of the truly great women writers—Jane Austen and George Eliot, to name two among the very greatest—are either dissected for the rightness or error of their attitudes, or simply violated to serve some political end. (Betty Friedan would no doubt take angry issue with my description of women's studies courses—just as she began at some point to deny that the movement was hostile to men—but perhaps had she interviewed as many women's studies majors who were looking for a job as I have, even she might have begun to wonder just what, aside from burnishing the young women's various hostilities, such courses are really doing for them. Needless to say, their professors are doing nicely, thank you.)

It was time, then, to sit down and try to think all this through. And as it happened, it was just about then that Willie Morris got himself, and ultimately the rest of us, pushed out of *Harper's*. So I had been freed to spend my time just reading and thinking about Women's Lib, and after a while, I decided I would write a book. Whereupon I bought, or where they were not for sale borrowed, every book, pamphlet, and manifesto put out by members of this movement: whether by the group attending elite colleges in the Northeast who called themselves the Redstockings, possibly, though it is a hard call, the most violent of all in their rhetoric; or by the leaders of NOW, hampered in their efforts to make a wide appeal to the women of America by the presence in their midst of a very active and vocal group of lesbians who were pursuing their own interests; or by the nonorganizational collection of poets, journalists, and would-be writers, who brought forth essays generally of the kind I quoted above. Some were better done than others, but all were positively choking with an indignation whose real source was not as easy as you might imagine to determine.

And there I was, reading and reading and taking careful notes and shaking my head with wonder. At one point, I came upon an essay written by a woman who had for a time been my husband's secretary. She described her growing disaffection with her job in his office and to my astonishment announced that she had acted out her rebellion on more than one occasion by pouring cups of coffee into her typewriter!

What were these women trying to tell us? They were saying

that they hated housework, which was no surprise—who in her right mind liked it?—only the violence of their feelings on the subject gave me pause. I could not, for one thing, get over the suspicion that those who complained the loudest were precisely the least conscientious housekeepers (like my complaining next-door neighbor in Glen Oaks—though she did have three babies in four small rooms). But whether or not my suspicion would have been borne out, from the very cadences in which the complainers expressed their disaffection, it seemed clear to me that something beyond mere stacks of dirty dishes was involved. The term commonly substituted for "housework" was "shitwork," which indicated that, as in the case of the girls in the radical student movement who rebelled against getting coffee, what bothered the women most about keeping house was not so much the actual work as the way everyone had simply assumed that it would be their responsibility.

There were, I thought, two sources for this resentment, one of them valid but the other almost pathological. The valid resentment stemmed from something that no one had yet begun to take the measure of, and that was that for some time a very large number of young women were being educated to lead what was basically the life of leisured gentlemen. With a few notable exceptions a girl who had no desire to be either a schoolteacher or a social worker would in those years elect to be a liberal arts major. In a society of growing affluence, the fields of teaching school and social work were no longer considered the essential thing for a girl to take up; in fact, they were coming more and more to be seen as female ghettos. A liberal arts education offers far better training to the sensibility but not a whole lot of training for anything else. All those lovely girl graduates who came every June to ask me for a job, or at least some advice about how and where to get one, were in a spot: they had studied art history or English or comparative literature or even philosophy and had actually been prepared to do nothing but cultivate their minds, if indeed that. Sooner or later they married, and must have done so with the natural expectation that they would lead interesting lives. But if they married well, they would have little or nothing to do, and if they married poor—a graduate student, say, or someone starting at the bottom—they would be likely to feel themselves unjustly burdened. Why should they be the ones to do dishes?

This was not their fault, or a benign society's fault either; it was just a condition that could not be cured—except, perhaps, with a sense of humor, something the Libbers were notably short of.

The second source of the sisterhood's bitterness about keeping house is the one that seemed to me to border on pathology, and that was the way they turned it into a zero-sum game with men: they had to clean and so on precisely because the men of the world had rigged it so that they were permitted to do nothing else. Assuming they were telling the truth, I don't know where or how all those liberationists came by such brutish mates. It had after all been not that long ago that I had lived in Glen Oaks, and many of the husbands there would come home after working all day followed by a brutal commute and do what they could to help out. (Many, though of course not all of them; but on the other hand, not all of the women would do much cleaning up either.)

The writer I cited above who was so bitter because her husband made a sexual advance to her while she was standing over the sink instead of pitching in and doing the dishes suggested that he did nothing all day while she was the one who had to go to work and then come home, fix dinner, and clean up. From what she says, he seems to have been a graduate student whom she was supporting and hence was no more than a parasitic lout. It occurred to me that maybe she didn't know many graduate students. At a certain point in my life I knew a lot of them, and oh God, what a sad lot most of them were, dragging themselves around trying to write their dissertations, afraid of their professors' power over their future, and all the while knowing that even after they had their Ph.D. degrees, they might have to go off to some unknown college in some far-off dinky town and begin working their way up. I would rather have washed sinkful after sinkful of dirty dishes than go through what they were going through. Perhaps that essayist had never asked her husband what he did all day.

And possibly, too, when he grabbed her to make love to her, it was far from the first time she had turned him away, and doing the dishes had been far from the only excuse. For if housework was the liberationists' bugaboo, what shall we say about sex? One of the first things to note about the movement's analysis of the traditional sexual transactions between women and men is the striking influence of lesbianism on it. Indeed, can one even say who came first—the resentful heterosexuals or the lesbians? Whatever is the answer, movement writings on the subject of sex are shot through with the idea that since prehistoric times men have been imposing on women their own standards of sexual behavior and erotic pleasure. First men demanded that their women be chaste so there would be no confusion about the paternity of their offspring, and recently, as if to stand the whole thing on its head, they contrived to unleash a sexual revolution in order to see to it that women, all women, would be easily available to them. It was this twofold male conspiracy, said the movement spokeswomen, that was to be tolerated no more. Moreover, one of the conspiracy's major impositions on women in modern times had been the sex experts' ideas about the vaginal orgasm—setting them off on a quest that would keep them both anxious and submissive. "Freud," wrote one of the movement's lesbian philosophers, "founded the myth of penis envy, and men have asked me 'But what can two women do together?' As though a penis were the sine qua non of sexual pleasure! Man, we can do without it, and keep it going longer too!"

It was not so much the vulgarity—although with an occasional rare exception, Erica Jong, for instance, women should be absolutely enjoined from writing about the sex act because they do it so grossly and witlessly—but the psychological and intellectual indelicacy with which they were characterizing women's experience that made me believe how injurious these women were becoming to the general welfare. If they had just been rash and violent like the students, one might have thought that they would grow out of it. But many of the women who chimed in, either in public or in private, had been around for a while, had husbands, lovers, fathers, children, and yet they seemed content to settle for the crassest caricatures of their own experience.

Movement-speak of any kind by its very nature involves a primitive rendering of reality. But neither of these circumstances by itself explains how it was that a friend of mine, a sweet, kind man whose work was a daily agony to him, twice a week came home from that work to find his living room occupied by a group of around a dozen women whose twice-weekly conversation was devoted to the subject of the piggishness of men and their various sufferings therefrom. Nor, as he described it, did this conversation sound in any way amused and salty as were those old front-steps chat sessions of the housewives of Glen Oaks. On the contrary, these women wept and grew angry and comforted one another—his wife, said my friend, the most vociferously of all. Two questions plagued him as he used to enter his house: what had he done? and was she talking this way to their two little daughters? Finally, it will not surprise anyone to hear, he stopped going home after work whenever he found the slightest excuse to stay away.

They called gatherings like that one, which had begun to take place in big cities across the country, "consciousness-raising." The concept had clearly been borrowed from group therapy, but the consciousness these sessions raised was certainly not intended, as in group therapy, to help those present come to any understanding of the role they played in the making of their own difficulties. On the contrary, its purpose was to count the ways in which they had been, and continued to be, the victims of society's, primarily men's, evil designs on them.

All this was supposed to come under the heading of feminism, this representation of women as the oppressed victims of persecution and rapine and false consciousness, kept in an inferior status, underpaid and unvalued except as servants. I myself had always thought of feminism as being true faith in, and admiration for, the nature and gifts and contributions of women.

I had certainly been brought up to admire my own mother: my father admired her, her siblings admired and depended on her, and the community in which she lived admired her. Had she been a professional, she would no doubt have been a highly regarded one. As it was, she did many different things and did them all well, and for a long time was felt to be a hard act to follow by my sisters and me. So in my view a feminist was someone who admired women and thought that in general they added a necessary and immeasurable value to whatever occupied them, whether at work or bringing up children or putting food on the table or even ironing sheets (though anyone who ever refused to do the latter has certainly had an ally in me).

There is no doubt that women's lives have been seriously altered over the course of the last two generations. They have decisive control over reproduction, they are no longer required to be sexually demure, and they are expected, and often required, to take care of themselves financially, at least for some time in their lives. This last is in a certain way the most critical for anyone who is by my lights a genuine feminist. For a woman to pursue a career means that she will be entering what was until only yesterday in historical terms, a man's world; and thus what she needs is both an understanding of the kind of commitment that will be required to make her way successfully in that world and an understanding that if she doesn't wish to make that commitment, it is perfectly all right, since what she might choose to do instead is vitally important. In other words, whatever it is she needs to do is to be valued and encouraged.

But the women's movement, the drummer so many women came to believe they had chosen to march behind, was telling them instead that they were people who had been deliberately kept down and that in order for them to succeed the whole system would have to be changed—if you will, revolutionized. This is the last thing in the world anyone should say to people who, if they need anything at all, need simple encouragement. Not, "You are a poor victim," but, "Of course, you can do it; just be patient and cheerful and give it time."

And if they were in pursuit of a new way of life in which they would require a new kind of comradeship from men, going to war against them was hardly a happiness-inducing way to achieve it.

The men, as we know, did not fight back; nor did they defend themselves. Some of them, like our friend who was afraid to pay our daughter a compliment lest she be offended, had merely surrendered and sued for peace. And a large number of them simply retreated behind some emotional redoubt where they could not be reached. Meanwhile, the movement that be-gan with the claim that it was out to make a real revolution in women's lives began to define the various forms of male with-drawal from combat as victories, whereas the truth was they were for the most part expressions of the deepest (and in most cases to this day unrecognized) contempt.

One night a few years after my immersion in the move-ment's philosophy I got myself involved in a fruitless argument over dinner with a man who happened to be the managing partner of a prestigious law firm. He was in essence accusing me of being insensitive to the sorrows of my fellow women—a charge that by then had grown wearyingly familiar to me. In the course of our discussion he mentioned that his firm had as a matter of principle hired several young female associates. "We don't make quite the same demands on their time," he added with what sounded to me like a certain sheepishness. When asked why not, he said, "Well, we recognize that their social life is terribly important to them."

With my much-vaunted insensitivity I wanted to go straight to his office the next morning and wring those young women's necks for playing into his patronizing hands this way. Of course, it was possible, if not indeed probable, that many of them had not been all that interested in the law in the first place: the time was the late seventies, and a lot of young women were marching into law school exactly the way they had once studied to be teachers, because of the pressure to do so in order to prepare themselves for a secure and well-paid career.

The sad truth is that women were now being patronized far and wide. In New York City, for instance, a group of them started an all-women's bank, which very quickly, and deservedly, failed. Why should women, who claimed to want to take their rightful place in the world, have a bank of their own, whose investors and depositors would participate merely because it was a woman's enterprise? This reasoning seemed to escape them, as it would the Ford Foundation, which agreed on a charitable basis to keep the bank open for a while. A somewhat better fate greeted the magazine, called *Ms.*, that was founded by a group of movement women. Though it, too, could never stand on its own feet, charitable support kept the magazine going for many years. To be sure, except for some of the fancy slicks and specialty publications, idea-driven magazines in general have not done well—it has become just too expensive to buy circulation and compete with TV for advertising—but *Ms.* was from the first issue on an amateurish operation, editorially as well as managerially, traveling exclusively on the fumes of its advocacy. In short, a double standard was being applied by a number of men to the enterprises of the women and by the movement's women to themselves as well.

But I get ahead of my story. Having studied carefully all the writings of Women's Liberation I decided to write a book about what this movement was actually up to. Most people seemed to view it, or perhaps pretended to view it, simply as a vehicle for combating discrimination. Equal pay for equal work, and all that. They nodded their agreement, or applauded, and shrugged nervously at any hint of a suggestion that something more might be involved. In those days everyone had grown used to anger as a mode of social analysis: after all, the raging antics of both the minority activists and the putatively rebellious youths had been viewed as merely a means of their "trying to tell us something" about injustice; so why not women?

Reading all those books and articles and pamphlets proved very enlightening. Trust not the artist, trust the tale, D. H. Lawrence once said. And by applying that principle, I came to see that one of the major things the movement women were up to was rebelling against the sexual revolution. But since attempting to get back to conditions before the onset of a revolution was by definition reactionary, they were out to achieve their liberation from liberation, so to speak, by moving forward. Which meant launching an all-out attack on men, their natures, their social behavior, and their sexual needs.

When it came to the issue of careers, what they demanded was not a chance to compete fairly but to turn the whole world of work upside down so as to make it more suitable to them. Marriage was to be a one-way deal—someone had even drawn up a model contract to ensure that husbands be made to signal their agreement to it—in which there would be no differentiation of "roles" between husband and wife. Men would share fully in the housework (those dirty dishes again) and baby care; and the fact that the husband might still be the primary breadwinner (the most famous of these contracts, for instance, was drawn up by a woman who happened to be a freelance writer) would count for nothing in the disposition of chores. Moreover, without such conditions, who needed marriage at all? Somehow it seems not to have occurred to any of these so badly put-upon women that if they really needed help of any kind from their husbands, rather than drawing up a formal contract, they might simply have tried asking nicely for it.

And as for children, in the movement's ideology they were

basically the enemy—considered alternately demanding and boring. There was some grudging recognition that women would continue to have children, but the conditions under which such a thing was to take place would have to be completely altered. One movement philosopher, Shulamith Firestone, looked forward to the day when children were born *ex utero* and saw no reason why such a day might not come soon. Others were not quite so radical, insisting only that once these babies were born, there be adequate universal daylong care for them. Gloria Steinem somewhere unforgettably expressed her resentment that anyone should expect her to consign herself to the intellectual company of a three-year-old, proving that she was pitiably unaware of either the charms or the brilliance of three-year-olds most particularly.

Beyond this catalog of errors were what I call the "trade-union" issues, that is, the by-now very famous demand for something called "equal pay for equal work." It was this demand, indeed, that drew many unsuspecting and right-minded women (my mother, for example) to express some degree of sympathy for the movement and at the same time gave millions of bewildered men a way to stay out of trouble, and politicians, a way to think of garnering some votes.

All this I wrote in my book (titled *The New Chastity* and published in 1972), in which I faithfully stuck to the movement's own sources and then compared it with the truths I knew on my own pulse about what women want and how they feel. I knew they genuinely hated the sexual revolution, for it is in women's nature to be monogamous; but on the other hand, whether or not their sexual experience was such as to earn the sexologists' approval, they want men to need *them* sexually, and to go on doing so. And as for babies, how much foresight did it take to predict that some day, having put it off for too long, a lot of not-quite-so-young women would grow panicked at the thought of being left childless?

Not surprisingly, the feminists assaulted me, and NOW even gave me its "Aunt Tom" award for the year. But what threw me off—to be honest, I should say put me off—was my discovery that I was left to stand virtually all alone. A few of my women friends whispered their agreement in corners while most males, including many of my dear friends, simply smiled vaguely and professed ignorance of the whole issue. I had thought that perhaps a few more of them might be emboldened to say something honest about their own feelings, but things had obviously gone too far for that. Those who did speak to me on the subject usually pawed the ground and told me I was being a little too tough on women like their wives and secretaries. Once I was invited by a professor of my acquaintance to speak to his class of young women at an all-female college. Afterward, I was invited to his house where I met his very handsome wife and two children, one a little boy of five or six, and one a baby only seven weeks old. As he drove me to the train, he complained to me that I was being insufficiently sympathetic to women's sufferings and told me a very sad tale about the sorrows of his old mother. He left me feeling troubled, because I did not think of myself as unsympathetic to the sorrows of women, old or young—or the sorrows of men either—and I thought long and hard about what he had said. Imagine my surprise, then, when only a month later a mutual friend announced to me that my erstwhile host had just left his wife and their two small children and run off with one of his students. No wonder he had professed so much sympathy for the troubles of women: it was a subject that he was at that very moment planning soon to have an active hand in.

The result of these charges against me was that I spent some time playing the requisite bad guy on discussion panels and was in that way vouchsafed many educative experiences. I learned that some people will boldly say things that neither they nor anyone else could possibly believe. I learned that when feminist leaders like Eleanor Smeal, for a long time the president of NOW, can't feign anger about something, they have nothing to say. And in an auditorium in the Middle West I heard Betty Friedan, by then a much-sought-after public speaker, actually declare to a large audience that she did not get orgasms from washing the kitchen floor. (Whereupon two questions immediately popped into my mind, first, doesn't anyone else ever flinch from the sheer tastelessness of this stuff as I do? And second, when in her entire life did this woman ever wash a kitchen floor?) But the main thing I learned was that this phenomenon so mistakenly called feminism would be here and doing untold damage to relations between the sexes for a long, long time.

≈ 5 ≈

Stormy Weather

WRITING A BOOK and carrying on a public debate was one thing, but I was also the mother of three daughters, two of whom by this time were young women and the third not very far from it. Talking to them about life and men and sex had nothing to do with politics or social analysis or ideology; this was a matter of my own children's lives and future welfare. Not only were they growing up in a culture that I believed had become increasingly dangerous for the young, but they were living in the very headwaters of that culture; in the case of Rachel and Naomi, in a posh private school and then in eastern private colleges, and in the case of their younger sister, Ruth, in a New York City public high school for students with a special gift for science—which, while not full of the socially privileged, amounted to the same thing when it came to "advanced" ideas.

Well, a good deal of the time I was quite hopeless in the

guidance department. I both did and desperately did not want to know about those girls' sex lives, for instance: because while I had very firm ideas in my own mind about the difficulty and emotional danger they would be letting themselves in for if they were to enjoy the kind of sexual license that was being extended to so many of their friends, I could not on the other hand simply fence them around in some kind of parietal never-never land. I neither had the power to do so nor would I have actually wished to do so. In those years especially, only fools could believe that they were succeeding in keeping their daughters locked up in some safe high tower, like Rapunzel in the fairy tale, where only their destined princes could brave the climb to find them.

My mother, who had been concerned that her daughters be what they used to call "popular"—or her own term for it, "well adjusted"—was at the same time very clear in her mind that they were to have as little experience as possible with boys. It was good to have dates with them—that was a mark of social success—but bad to make even the slightest show of intimacy. In other words, my sisters and I were being held to what you might call contradictory expectations.

For someone like me—a public intellectual engaged in public debate on this very question—things could never be quite so simply compartmentalized. Not that I was free of a certain contradiction of my own. I wanted to keep my girls protected—it was a dangerous world out there—but I knew it would be foolish to expect that they would not venture at all, sexually speaking. Everything and everyone around them offered encouragement to the pretense of emotional and sexual precocity. Still, I could see with the naked eye that worldly sophistication at too young an age, in addition to damaging a young girl's sense of the openness and even mystery of the future, was plain enervating. Some of my daughters' friends who visited our house were already behaving like weary older women, and I sometimes felt like crying to see them that way when they should have been lively blooming young creatures. Some of these girls had engaged themselves in those monogamous pseudomarriages, which kept them feeling safe, at least for a time (and that must have seemed to their boyfriends at first an unbelievable piece of good luck but after a while must have also become something of a drag, for in exchange for the steady availability of sex they were required to behave like little old husbands before they had, as it were, even begun to shave). But all this was so upside down and unfair: it should have been the society surrounding those girls, and not a series of pretend marriages, that kept them feeling safe and so enabled them to try their wings and feel their power—and champ at the bit to greet the future as the young are supposed to do.

But how could I communicate any of this except in words, and in far too complicated words at that? So I would talk and talk, talk their heads off, talk till their eyes rolled around in their heads from boredom. When it came time for her turn, Ruth, the last of the three, would put up an argument—it was in her nature—but the two older ones would simply wait patiently for the torrent to slacken off so they could politely beat a retreat. Or perhaps they were listening after all? I don't know. It is highly doubtful that I would have been listening (or even polite) had I been in their shoes.

One of the things I tried to talk to them about was boys, or if you will, men. For the deadly explosive mixture of the sexual revolution and the women's movement had combined not only to poison relations between the sexes—women explosively complaining and men silently seething with resentment—but to becloud any understanding of what, beneath the changing tides of fashion, sex is all about: namely, that men pursue and women decide whether or not to surrender. It is, I suppose, a game, but a game that is especially hazardous for a woman to lose, for sex makes babies, and she needs her babies to be fathered. In the end, she offers him an unspoken deal: you cleave unto me, forsaking all others, and be father to my babies, and I promise that I will repay this violation of your sexual nature, which is to be promiscuous, by making you a home and in other ways making it worth your while.

But hazardous as the game of sex may be for a woman, it is also not without danger for a man. Reject him and his pride will suffer, but remove from him the taste of power in the pursuit, and some essential part of his energy will be sapped. By pretending that men and women are alike sexually—as the sexual revolution did—or that women's needs in marriage are at least to begin with not greater than men's—as the women's movement did—sex is not a properly played game in which everyone wins but a struggle with no rules in which everyone loses.

I could not, I knew, referee my daughters' playing of this game—and truth to tell, I would rather have died than try. Moreover, I also knew perfectly well that they could not play alone, that is, if the boys were not going to be manly, the girls would find it very difficult, if not impossible, to be womanly. But the boys with whom they went to school or whom they encountered within the general precincts of their society were being brought up to be anything but manly. To take a small but not insignificant example, I had tried to establish the simple rule that if the girls were going out with a young man, they were to be picked up and brought home. This rule seemed to me not only a minimal demand but a very practical one, since traveling around the streets of Manhattan at night was not necessarily a safe thing for a young girl to do by herself. My daughters moaned in protest: they knew it would never happen. But I tried to keep the pressure on anyway, because if the boys wouldn't be men, I still wanted the girls to treat themselves for what they actually were, namely, young women in need of protection. I also wanted them to understand that in the end males do not thrive, even sexually, on a regimen of ho-hum sex, for it is pursuit, courtship, that gives them energy, including erotic energy. Among the boys they knew, the only ones who seemed to me to be on their way to being men were the ones who had not yet worked up the nerve to take on the girls. Why was this? Perhaps because they had more of themselves invested in some future goal—what the experts used to call "deferred gratification." All this I tried to say to them in long nighttime conversations while they, mannerly as they always were, waited me out.

Beyond the question of my feeble attempts to give them a putatively unenlightened lesson in a highly enlightened manner, there is the larger question of the general nature of my mothering. Would dealing with sex have been easier for any of the four of us females if throughout their early adolescence I had been at home every day to greet them with a glass of milk and a hug? Probably so. Life would unquestionably have been a good deal easier all around for my son John, who was at the time of which I write just leaving childhood and entering that no-man's-land, pre-pre-adolescence, a time of incalculable unease, especially for a little boy. But in any case something worse was happening to them than my being absent until dinnertime: namely, they were being educated about life by me and my husband in one way and at the same time being kept by us in the special New York literary world where a whole lot of what we told them was being contradicted by everything they saw.

This was, for instance, a time of parties. We all had parties, some dinner parties, some big ones (one New Year's Eve, my husband and I decided to invite simply everybody we knew— God alone knows how many people showed up). And at these parties, in addition to a lot of very sophisticated attitudinizing, everyone drank a great deal and sometimes became quite unruly. There were always heady arguments and headier flirtations and expressions of the most advanced attitudes about everything. This was the world with which our children were totally familiar and whose standards and attitudes they were at the same time being constantly warned against by their parents.

Which was, to use the indispensable locution of children everywhere, "no fair"—and monumentally so.

Ultimately even we, who were grown up and well armed, found it impossible to retain our citizenship in literary New York; so what of our children? The four of them reacted to this imposition on them very differently from one another. Rachel walked around through high school with a ten-ton burden on her shoulders. Eventually she took herself off to Israel to live in a kibbutz near the northern border where she tended the children and learned a few things about real danger. Naomi, she who would not be conned, would also take herself off to Israel in her junior year of college, intending to finish school at the Hebrew University and come back home to America, which she did. She, the ostensibly unimpressionable one, had originally been smitten with the place in the course of one of those one-month summer youth tours, from which she returned filled with Vietnam-time envy for her Israeli counterparts. As we were walking through the airport on her return, she turned to me and demanded, "Do you know what it is *like* to be in a place where the people love the soldiers?" "Yes," I told her, "I do. It was like that in this country once, before you were born." Then Ruth, number three daughter, followed in her elder sister's footsteps, and she, too, finished college in Israel—and, in the end, met a young man, married him, and remained there permanently.

How far they had to journey, my three girls, to enjoy the sensation that life, life in general and each of their lives in particular, was a serious matter.

My son, John, the youngest, was a rather different story. He was only fourteen when the United States finally bugged out of Vietnam, so most of his adolescence was spent in a somewhat different atmosphere where the country in general was concerned. A lot of people would be trying to get over the shame of watching those films of the helicopters leaving the roof of the American embassy with South Vietnamese hanging on to them and begging to be taken as well—a sight bound to have moved the hearts even of the editors of *Rolling Stone* magazine. The Democrats, who had after all taken us into that ambivalently executed war, had been diverting themselves with the spectacle of their most hated enemy, Richard Nixon, completely self-destructing over a mysterious piece of idiocy called Watergate. Most of the universities were by then lying quietly in shambles, victims of their own passivity in the face of the student resistance. And some of the young men who had dodged the draft were beginning to feel the first twinges of the shame that a few of them would be speaking of in public in a decade's time.

But as for our son, his most serious introduction to the fact that we were facing new times would be provided him right in his own home. For no longer would his parents be members in good standing of the community that had so clearly represented the contradiction in the center of our daughters' lives. On the contrary, my husband and I were now at war with that community, a war actually declared and consciously fought in the pages of *Commentary*, of which my husband had for some years by then been the editor in chief.

For in the course of the sixties we had grown more and more disgusted by, and contemptuous of, both the heedless and mindless leftist politics and intellectual and artistic nihilism of fashionable literary-intellectual society. We had opposed the war but could not bear the way so many of our anti–Vietnam War comrades were hoping not merely for an end to the war but for the victory of our country's enemies. We were disgusted by the plain unholy ingratitude of some of our very, very fortunate friends and acquaintances who professed to see no difference between the United States and the Soviet Union. And we were dead set against the kind of contemptuous racism that led so many liberals to demand special allowances for the criminal behavior of blacks.

Added to this litany, or perhaps in my case the very first item on it, was my recognition that living as I had been, and where I had been, I had been subjecting my own children to danger: the danger that they would be worn down and jaded before they had ever had the chance, or the spiritual wherewithal, to take on the chills and spills of real adulthood. Put these feelings and ideas all together, and they amounted to what would one day come to be called neoconservatism.

To begin with, this break was extremely painful for both of us. Naturally it did not happen overnight but was cumulative, which meant first some difficulty with this friend and then a quarrel with that one. We ceased to be invited to a lot of places and for our part turned down invitations that were extended to us. One of the things that eased our passage out of the New York literary world was a new political life with a group of people younger than we whose passions were not literary but political and who were not "liberals," as that term had been corrupted to mean, but rather social democrats. They had been fighting the campus radicals in the name of anti-Communism, pro-Americanism (especially in Vietnam), and loyalty to George Meany's labor movement (which was also anti-Communist and pro-American, including with respect to Vietnam). To be a social democrat in those years meant to be to the right of the Democratic party and to the left of the Republican party: a very narrow place, where neither we nor the labor movement could permanently remain. Ultimately the union membership would tire of its social democratic leaders and allow itself to be moved straight left. Most of the rest of this odd group, distinguishable primarily for being that which was the most unpopular of all in our former literary world—namely simple patriots—when the time came would fly into the arms of Ronald Reagan. From there it would be only a short and easy journey into full-blown conservatism.

Like his older sisters, our son also attended school in the liberal heartland, but at least he no longer had to deal with the contradictions to which his older sisters had been subjected in the social life at home. On the other hand, in addition to having been put at odds with the culture of his everyday world, he had taken upon himself, even when he was a little squirt, the heavy burden of being brave. One day during the 1972 presidential campaign, for instance, the children were asked by the guest speaker in a school assembly who among them would, if he were old enough, vote for Richard Nixon. John, eleven years old, raised his hand and, as he had probably guessed he would be, was the only one in that whole auditorium full of kids to do so. (His teachers later told us how much they had admired him for doing that, without appearing to have considered that there might be something wrong with their teaching, or with the school in which they were doing that teaching, for there to be such perfect unanimity of political attitude among several hundred children.) But though, as I said, times were changing, everywhere he turned there would still be a whole lot of culture inimical to what he believed. From the earliest age he had been a performing arts man, especially mad for movies and the theater. Still, while he had a passion for everything and everybody that moved upon the stage or screen, something in him also had to resist much of what they were saying and doing. This is a proper position to be in for the movie and theater critic he ultimately became but was surely something of a burden for the young boy he was.

And as I write this, it occurs to me that there should have been some form of special hazard pay for the job of being our children.

In the end, our daughters' difficulties turned out to be far from as great as those faced by many of the young women they had gone through school with. It is harrowing to remind oneself of the wreckage visited upon the children of the famous baby boom who grew up among the so-called enlightened classes. Just among the circle of my daughters' acquaintance there were girls consigned to psychiatric hospitals, others in and out of drug treatment programs, one who spent several years shut up in her bedroom from which she might or might not emerge for meals, and some who attended one or another of the most prestigious all-girls colleges opted out of the whole struggle by joining one of the groups of lesbians on hand to recruit them. Lesbianism being something it is possible to outgrow—as homosexuality is evidently not—it seems possible that some of the college lesbians who were simply hiding from engagement with men changed their sexual style at some point later in life. But in the meanwhile, they were undoubtedly members in good standing of the chorus heaping contumely on males, while the nearby males stood around wondering where and how to go about lifting the indictment that had been brought against them. Let us just say, in a gross understatement, that these were far from the safest or healthiest of times to be a young woman, or a young man either.

I found it difficult to speak to my son about these things. Being a young boy whose two oldest sisters for a long time regarded him as a kind of plaything, and his third, as an interloping enemy, he was not inclined to believe that females understood him or took him sufficiently seriously. From one point of view this was good, for what females in those days were automatically given to saying about males—all males, or, if you will, the male principle—was not something that any mother could have wished for her young son to absorb. But it was naturally also bad, because any boy of his class who would not agree to be what with a terribly crude precision is called pussy-whipped was bound to be left feeling alienated. How could I discuss this with him from what would have looked to him to be my great age and enviably safe perch? Besides, I believed then and believe even more today that it is for a boy's father to talk to him about girls. Anyway, unlike the way things were with his sisters, by the time he got to college the worst of the terrible sixties and seventies was over. True, the boy-girl thing was still in a shambles, while the homosexual rights movement was busy carrying off some of the most seriously wounded from the feminist battleground. But at least drugs and radicalism were no longer the only show in town. Indeed, something new was happening: the second tranche of neoconservatives were coming of age, unburdened with a messy past and full of beans.

But before all that was to happen to John and his buddies,

there had in my opinion been a lot of work for us elders to do. Just as I had earlier felt the need to understand what had gone so bitterly wrong in the lives of America's privileged women, I also came to feel a greater pressure to try to figure out how things had gone so bitterly wrong with so many of America's healthy, apparently well-tended, and advantaged children. The question came upon me most urgently one day when I received news that a handsome and intelligent young girl whom I had not seen since she was an early adolescent was living in a commune and had just given birth to her first, naturally illegitimate, baby and was giving her one of those marijuana-induced names so popular in those days—Moonbeam, or Jagger, or something on that order.

I had heard earlier about this girl when she had dropped out of college and moved to San Francisco to be a Buddhist, a state of affairs her parents explained to me with these words, "It doesn't happen to be our way of life, but it does happen to be hers." They were fine and thoughtful progressive people, these parents, good citizens and good neighbors. They had not fought with her when she dropped out of school and they would certainly not fight with her or disown her now, when she had presented them with a grandchild. That her life might sooner or later be a miserable one, and that of their grandchild even more so, they did not allow to enter their minds, so busy feeling "enlightened" were they. Anyway, the day I was informed of the birth of little Moonbeam—or whatever—a number of thoughts that had been rattling around in my mind suddenly came together, and I sat down and began to write a book, a book that would in the end be titled *Liberal Parents, Radical Children*.

The thesis of this book was that the offspring born to the most "enlightened" sector of my generation, who had as no babies before them been cosseted and petted, whose bodies had been cared for and minds stimulated, so to speak, within an inch of their lives, were in the end neglected children. They were neglected in all sorts of ways. Many of them, for instance, had been left virtually mannerless, slouching into one's house without a hello and slouching out again without a good-bye, the girls unable to manage introductions of their male companions, and the boys, as I said, completely untutored about their responsibility to their female companions. When they arrived home late at night with pupils so dilated they virtually covered their entire eyes, their parents asked pleasantly and oh-so-liberally if they had had a good time. (Like my mother's injunction to be "popular," these kids were constantly being enjoined to have a "good time"—the questions "Did you have a good time at school today?" and later, "Did you have a good time at the party?" indicating the need for assurance not that the kid was actually enjoying himself but that his parents didn't have to worry too much about him.)

I had felt the urge to write a book about all this, but for the longest time I could not figure out how. There were no texts to guide my argument, as there had been in the case of Women's Lib, and on the other hand, the last thing on earth I wished or felt entitled to do was write a long sermon. And then, like an unexpected gift, it was the announcement of the birth of little Moonbeam that all at once opened the floodgates. I sat down and at white heat wrote a little essay called "A Letter to the Young," and when it was finished, I realized that it was the introduction to the book I had been struggling to shape in my mind.

⁓ 6 ⁓

Coming Out

HAVING A BOOK in one's typewriter can be a lonely business. Each day you send a little bucket down into the well and wonder what you will send up to yourself. Sometimes it will be a gift, and sometimes it will be a joke—on you, that is. When I was writing *Liberal Parents, Radical Children,* only John was left at home. He was in junior high school and often away until late afternoon, so what was inevitably lonely became lonelier still, and quieter than I think I had ever known a house to be in my entire life. And never again would my home be as tidy, or my kitchen floor as clean, or our dinners as lengthily prepared, as in the year I was working on that book.

When it was finished, I didn't know what to do with myself; I couldn't, after all, mop the floor twice every afternoon. Nor did I wish to spend my time exclusively suffering over the composition of book reviews and magazine articles as a freelancer: I had just put in my time at the typewriter and was dying to leave that snug little prison I had created for myself where my desk stood cheek by jowl with the ironing board.

At a dinner party I ran into an acquaintance named Erwin Glikes, who was then in the process of becoming the wonder boy of serious book publishing. He had recently been made head of a small publishing company called Basic Books, and he asked me if I would like to come work there as an editor. I told him I knew nothing about book publishing, to which he answered that there was very little to learn, I could pick it up in a couple of weeks. I knew he was lying in his teeth. Erwin was a seducer; it was his MO, as the crime busters say. But it had been so many years since anyone had put the moves on me that I said yes. And so began my (short-lived) career in book publishing.

To begin with, naturally, I was a complete novice. After a while—though certainly far from a mere couple of weeks—I began to make sense of such things as how to price a book and estimate a print run and before that, for openers, something as elementary as the meanings of words as they were used in the professional lingo. But at bottom the real difficulty was that I was now for the first time in an actual business, devoted to making profit and answerable to investors. I realized the difference the very first time I proposed that we publish a certain book that I was enthusiastic about, written by a clever and fascinating woman whose previous work I had admired. Who is going to buy this book? I was asked, and hadn't the faintest idea how to answer. It often used to be said that publishing in its glory days had been largely the preserve of leisured gentlemen, for whom such questions as I had been asked had played little part in the making of publishing decisions. And even so, by the time William Faulkner won the Nobel Prize for literature, hardly any of his books—maybe only the oddity called *The Wild Palms*—were in print. And here I was with a nice, clever book, being asked to justify someone's investment—printing, paper, binding, marketing, and royalty—of many thousands of dollars on my own say-so.

What on earth had I done to myself? Nearly fifty years old and starting all over again like a kid! Erwin was amused, but I was not.

Meanwhile, as low man on the totem pole, and still waiting for the books I had contracted for to be finished, I was given the job of doing Erwin's rejections. He was, shall we say, an exuberant responder to ideas for books and rather less exuberant about dealing with his own mistakes when the fleshed-out proposals or first chapters arrived on his desk. And what is the point of being a boss if you have to do your own dirty work? This particular duty made me some new enemies, but by then I had already made myself a goodly number of my own as a writer, so most of the fear had already gone out of having a few more.

And while it would take me some time really to learn my way around, there were a couple of things I knew that no one else in that firm seemed to. I knew, for one thing, what it felt like to be a writer, and I would sometimes storm around the office at the sight of a pile of manuscripts that had been contracted for and then left untouched and unread for weeks, maybe months. Has it come to your attention that there is a real live person at the other end of that pile of paper? I would demand, like a schoolmarm or librarian with a pencil in her knotted hair. And now and then my preachments would have some effect. I also knew what it felt like to be edited, and to be told by someone that what I had written suffered from certain shortcomings without his being able to tell me what exactly he meant or how to fix it: which may be one of the purest forms of anxiety known to man. I also lectured on this point constantly, but, I fear, with rather less success.

I had one colleague, for instance, who was known to be very distinguished in the field of serious book publishing (and who when Erwin Glikes left us to dive into a bigger pond would for a brief time become my boss), who may single-handedly have caused more anxiety attacks among would-be authors than the whole rest of the industry combined. He was, as they say, a lovely man, but he could not make up his mind, nor having made it up, communicate what was on it to any author. Nor, decent in his instincts as he was, could he do much better as a boss.

(Eventually two things would drive me out of book publishing: the decision to act on a long-smoldering political passion was one, and he was the other.)

Because of my magazine experience I simply took for granted that it was part of my job to edit manuscripts—I mean actually to edit them, line by line, page by page. In most publishing houses nowadays, what we in the magazine business used to call editing is not often engaged in by editors; at Basic Books it certainly wasn't by anyone but me. Rather it is often a function performed by underpaid women in the back room or farmed out to even more severely underpaid women who work freelance at home. Unlike them, however, because I was the one in direct contact with the authors, I knew when to ease up with the blue pencil and when to bear down. So rather than be the middleman between an author and his copy editor (and anyway not all the ladies in the back room were as literate as they might be, and as, indeed, they were once famous for being), I did the job myself.

There was another reason for doing the job myself, and that

was . . . the feminists. Because it was an axiom of the business that women were predominantly the book buyers (and Jewish women at that), and because the majority of the young women employed in publishing were graduates of the "better" colleges—where feminism reigned—the movement had moved in on the industry in a big way. They managed to convince the powers that be that what displeased them would be bad for business, and what is in a sense at least as important, they managed to take control of the English language. They issued guidelines of acceptable usage which made their way into every copy department and thus positively barbarized the language of a large number of books, especially in the fields of psychology, political science, and social analysis. In a way the worst, because the most common, form of barbarity was the abrogation of the use of "he" in stating the general case. Every literate person knows that this use of the masculine carries no intention to exclude women but is a mere convention, no doubt settled on in ages long past for the sake of brevity and grace. For those who abide strictly by the new guidelines, however, the general case must be stated by means of the use of "he/she," or what may be worse, "s/he"—something that could even take the poetry out of Shakespeare. Yet there "he/she" is, spattered over countless books and setting countless teeth on edge.

Another feminist corruption was the interdiction of the use of the word "girl" or "girls" to refer to any female virtually beyond her days in the sandbox. This was clearly derived from the feminist movement's aping of the civil rights movement: because the word "boy" had been one of the racists' ways of expressing their abiding contempt in addressing black men, by the same token the word "girl" was now ruled out as an insult to womankind.

Some of all this makes one merely shake one's head, such as

hearing history referred to as "herstory" or, more commonly, hearing God referred to as "She." But some of it makes one despair for an already dwindling literacy. We were known to many people, mistakenly, as a politically conservative publishing house because we did not simply rule out, but rather made a fair amount of money from, conservative books. And our copy editors were actually quite conservative when it came to such things as English usage, though it must be said that even they could not totally resist the tide. And one day there turned up a new one, a young man, who sat down and went through a wise and beautiful manuscript about blind children written by Selma Freiberg and murdered it, sentence by sentence, page by page. That's what he had been taught to do at his previous job, under the tutelage of some fierce and unforgiving woman, and that is what he assumed he was to do with us. Feeling rather fierce and unforgiving myself, I made him erase every correction, but he had been too badly beaten up by women in his past to be able to desist from their guidelines, and happily one day he simply disappeared from the office, never to return.

An equally significant problem in the field of publishing in those days, however, came not from the choke-hold over language that the feminists were maintaining but from the new female college graduates. I mentioned earlier that when I was in the magazine business, I used to see many of these girls every June, just come to town and hoping to find "interesting" work, but that was nothing compared with my experience in the office of a book publisher. This was no longer an army but a horde: lovely, attractive, well-turned-out girls without real skills and by and large without any passionate interest in acquiring any.

Not long after this time the situation would begin to change rather rapidly, as ambitious girls would now be marched by the pressure of feminist convention into law school, business school, and, to a somewhat lesser degree, medical school. But until that was to happen, there they were, basically young ladies of leisure, their heads full of dreams of an elegant, high-toned career—dreams planted in them during their years at Smith, Wellesley, Bryn Mawr, Harvard, et al.—marching into my office and out again. Eventually some of the particularly good-looking and clever—or the very well-connected—ones would find themselves a not-shameful berth in publishing or public relations, and most of the rest would go on to graduate school to study psychology or fine arts. But wherever they ended up, most of them would continue to harbor hopes, un-recognized as such, of an old-time-y gentlemanly existence. And the impossibility of such hopes in the United States of America in the 1970s is what sent so many of them, restless and resentful, into the arms of the women's movement.

For their younger sisters, those pressed to march in a straight line into what had been formerly thought of as primarily men's professions, there would of course be very little leisure in either becoming or being lawyers and stockbrokers and doc-tors. The work was long and hard, and the opportunity to make some serious money was very real (although we are told by the keepers of data that the overwhelming number of women doctors go into the least remunerative end of the pro-fession, i.e., family medicine). Nevertheless, without their real-izing it, there was something almost as sheeplike in their taking up these careers as there had once been in the desire to "go into" publishing. It was the thing to do for a young woman who had been pressed into declaring her independence of, and competitiveness with, father, brother, and potential husband. Once upon a time long ago girls had become schoolteachers and social workers, urged on by Depression-time parents who were for obvious reasons obsessed with security. Now the pressure on them comes not from their parents (who are torn between feelings of pride in their achievements and anxiety about their happiness) but from the limited and limiting feminist definition of self-respect. This had already begun to happen little by little during the time that I was being a book editor, but would begin to reach full velocity in the following decade.

As for me, by the time of my sojourn at Basic Books I had had a variety of jobs in a variety of places, but—with the exception of *Harper's,* pulled out, as it were, from under me—in none of them did I somehow feel settled. Early in my working life, I had been desperate for money: first as the wife of a graduate student whom I was helping to support, later as a divorcée with two children whose ex-husband was not exactly lavish with his child support and whose parents believed that I should lie in the bed I made for myself. There is something very good about working under the great pressure of the immediate need for money, for whether you like what you are doing or not, it counts enormously, and every little improvement is an achievement. Men who support their families, no matter how grim the circumstances under which they do so, must have this experience. So it was that later, when I married my second husband and he without question took fully upon himself the burden of being the paterfamilias while what I was earning was not quite covering the cost of having a housekeeper, going to work lost its savor. Thus when I decided to go back into the labor market, I would no longer be a needy and hence grateful kid, and my demand on the job would be that it had to repay my being away from home.

That demand would by its very nature turn out to be none too easy to fulfill. And when Willie tanked at *Harper's* and took the rest of us with him, I had been up against it: either some imaginary prince would ride by on his steed to rescue me or I would have to bow to the wishes of my real prince at home and be a full-time writer. A fate worse than death, it seemed to me then, but while my husband was willing to put up with my gibbering every night, I could at that point think of no alternative. What followed then was my book about the women's movement, which I had to spend more time defending than I had spent in writing.

Then out of the blue came a phone call from the much celebrated Norman Cousins, a man whom I had never met before, and he was asking me to be the managing editor of his new magazine. Against my husband's urging, I said yes. And just as my husband had predicted, this arrangement lasted a brief unhappy time for both Cousins and me, because we agreed on nothing: neither politics, nor writing, nor editing, nor even layout. One evening we decided in the friendliest fashion that the arrangement hadn't worked out; I acceded to his request to run the magazine's book review section from my house until a replacement could be found; and once more returned home—this time to face writing the book about the sixties young.

At that point, far, far too late, I formulated an employment policy for myself: to wit, I would never again work for anyone whom I would not hire to work for me.

And then came Erwin Glikes. . . .

This is without question the saga of a deeply restless woman—the result of the simple fact that I couldn't bear to sit by myself for too long in front of my typewriter. Now and then I would be moved to write an essay; now and then I would be asked to review a book; but to depend on one or the other or both of these to occupy my energies—in other words, to become a full-time freelance writer—was a prospect that for many years would send a chill down my spine.

But there was something else besides that old confrontation with the typewriter that kept me so uneasy in all these jobs, that kept me, in other words, from digging in and making a serious and steady career of any one of them, and that was the fact that my working was not essential to the support of the household. Naturally, the money I made came in very handy, especially with all that school tuition to pay, but it was not, in that other life-and-death way, necessary. I had once stuffed envelopes all day, and another time sold slips in a bargain store, with perfectly good cheer because my doing so was at the time helping to keep food on the family table. But being married now to a man who insistently and without complaint took upon himself the task of looking after us all in a far better than merely decent way, I found myself sniffing at jobs others would have envied. Maybe that was why so many feminists insisted that being the family breadwinner did not entitle a man to any special consideration: because without the pinch of necessity as a goad, work for pay was deprived of its most important satisfaction. And maybe, too, that's why they became so status-mad, carrying on about breaking what they called the "glass ceiling" that kept them from the executive suite, as if the executive suite were some garden of hidden daylong pleasures.

Book publishing had certainly not been without satisfactions. Being responsible for a book that made a great deal of money—like George Gilder's *Wealth and Poverty* or Robert Bork's *The Antitrust Paradox* and two or three by Thomas Sowell—was certainly a new and major one of these. And even more than the joys of having been responsible for a successful enterprise there were the friendships with certain authors that turned out to be lifelong ones. But publishing's days, too, were numbered as far as I was concerned. Aside from the fact that I was working too hard, making far too little money, and being driven crazy by the nice man who took over after Erwin left, publishing itself had begun to present me with a more pressing problem: I had become an ardent ideologue, moved by what I considered to be the calamitous cultural and political developments of the preceding decade—and I found that with every passing year I was growing ever more restless to get directly into the fray. I had been publicizing my views, to be sure, in my two books and in numerous magazine articles and op-ed pieces as well. But writing is one thing—one lonely thing—and I began to be moved by the itch to get involved in something more activist.

In the spring and summer of 1976 I had actually worked as a volunteer in two political campaigns—for the Democratic presidential nomination of Henry M. Jackson and the first senatorial nomination of Daniel Patrick Moynihan. Jackson lost and Moynihan won; but election campaigning itself held, and holds, little attraction for me: being involved in electioneering is neither a fitting nor a comfortable activity for an ideologue.

But neither, it turned out, was publishing. One morning about three years after those campaigns, I had an experience that really brought home to me how truly unsuited I had become to being in a publishing house. Basic Books had brought out a book called *The Romance of American Communism* by a leftist writer named Vivian Gornick. The book was a series of portraits of old American Commies, and it was full of nostalgia and high sentiment. The only character who was portrayed as unattractive was a man who had turned against the crimes of Stalin, and soon after had left the Communist party. Now, if you work for a book publisher, you are supposed to pray for the success of all the books published by your publishing house; but on this particular morning when I opened the *New York Times* and discovered that its daily reviewer had slammed Miss

Gornick's book, I cheered. Actually sat at the breakfast table sipping my coffee, and cheered. How, after everything any reasonable person should have known by then about Communism, could we have put out such a book? I shouted. And then: a fine member of the house of Basic you are, I said; you are clearly in the wrong business.

The right business would one day, at long last, present itself, but not until a number of other changes had been rung in my political and intellectual life. Those campaigns in 1976 were my first, but they did not constitute the beginning of my activist life. That had taken place four years earlier when Richard Nixon was competing for his second presidential term with George McGovern. McGovern's candidacy signalized the capture of the Democratic party by the hard Left, who had taken control of it through a lethal combination of radical opposition to the war in Vietnam, the radicalization of the civil rights movement, and Women's Liberation. Even in the heat of the Vietnam War, no radical or representative of radicals could ever win the presidency of the United States, so there was clearly no possibility of a McGovern victory. But there were a group of us Democrats who in a state of combined fear and disgust about what had become of the Democratic party viewed the inevitable McGovern defeat as our opportunity to recall the Democrats to their commitments to the policies, as we put it, of Franklin D. Roosevelt, Harry Truman, and John F. Kennedy. Among us were moderate activists from the camps of Hubert Humphrey, the true father of civil rights legislation and vice president to Lyndon Johnson, and Henry M. "Scoop" Jackson, senator from Washington and the leading liberal advocate of a firm anti-Soviet policy and a strong American defense; previously nonactivist intellectuals like my husband and me and several others; and a group of young intellectual workers in the vineyards of the labor movement. By the time McGovern had gone down to one of the worst defeats in the country's history, we were ready with a publicized statement of purpose which said in effect that we were opposed to the Left and to all those legislative and judicial measures—for a primary example, affirmative action—whose intent was to overturn the country's essential philosophical and political underpinnings. We called ourselves the Coalition for a Democratic Majority, or CDM, and, to put it mildly, nothing serious ever followed from what seemed to us like a most auspicious beginning (except, again, for a number of lifelong friendships). The then-leadership of the AFL–CIO, which provided a significant part of our meager treasury, were certainly sympathetic but were at that point far too occupied with opposing Nixon to lend us any real power. Our purposes were further diluted by a few members of the Humphrey group who thought that since the Left in the person of George McGovern had been thoroughly defeated, it was time to make peace with them. But mainly—a crucial lesson if your game is politics—you cannot get into that particular game without a candidate; and foolishly our candidate, Senator Jackson, felt it was not yet in his interest to offer himself to us. So CDM basically withered on the vine, and in 1976 the Democrats, unreformed, took back the White House from Nixon-Ford with Jimmy Carter. During all this time CDM hosted an occasional banquet and handed out an occasional award, but our success as an influence on the Democratic party may be measured by the fact that Carter had appointed only one lonely member of the group to any position in his administration, and that was an ambassadorship to some faraway and forgettable land about which we and the rest of our fellow Americans knew, and cared, nothing.

But one snowy late-winter morning in 1980 at God knows

whose urging President Carter invited the leaders of CDM to
the White House, the idea evidently being that he would have
to run for office again that year and maybe he could use a little
support from the moderates in his party. So a group of us met
with him, and a silly meeting it was. This president of the
United States, by whose own account it took the Soviet inva-
sion of Afghanistan to teach him more about the Soviet Union
than he had ever known, evidently forgot that the purpose of
our invitation to the White House was to court us for support
in the upcoming presidential election. On the contrary, he
clearly expected us to court him. He became visibly annoyed
when we offered him what was less obeisance than he expected
and demanded, and soon walked off with flaming cheeks and
left us to the ministrations of his staff. One of our number that
day was Jeane Kirkpatrick. As we left the White House we
were approached by the group of TV reporters who seem to
hang out on the White House lawn every day waiting for
something to happen; and—as it would turn out for all of us,
fatefully—she faced the cameras and announced that she was
going to support Ronald Reagan.

The truth is, Carter had been right to respond to us as he
had, because with only one or two exceptions the delegation
that met with him that day had by then lost all interest in saving
the Democratic party: not only because it had not changed but
because we had. For a group of us CDM had turned out to be
a kind of last-ditch effort to hang on to the liberalism that had
been to that point our lifelong estate. We are the real liberals,
we kept insisting; those others who have usurped and sullied
the good name of liberalism have to be identified for what they
are, namely, radicals, people beyond the pale of proper politics.

But all the while we were saying that, we were actually
moving to the Right, which was precisely what the logic of

our position dictated. For in the end you cannot defend American democracy without defending the economic system that is its necessary underpinning. And you cannot truthfully defend that system, called capitalism,[1] without accepting a number of other propositions, perhaps the principal one being that government should be restricted from interfering in lawful economic activity. Paul Johnson, who is among various other admirable things a great modern historian, has said that once he understood that socialism was wrong, he had to rethink everything he knew, including even what he knew about the Roman empire.

Well, perhaps without going so far as all the way back to the Roman empire, we, too, had to rethink most of what we had once thought, not only about politics but about a whole slew of things that fall under the category of what you might call the Nature of Man and God.

For me in particular, what I had seen moving in the culture of this country beginning in about 1965 had been like an arrow aimed at the nervous system. Because the preparation of this explosion from the decade before was something I myself had had a hand in. Or if it seems too self-aggrandizing for me to put it that way, I will just say the preparation for the sixties explosion was something I had all too carelessly embraced, as a way, it strikes me now, of continuing to assert my membership in the gang of the bad kids who refused to mind their mothers. My children were small then, and I had recklessly failed to make any connection between the fun of playing around in my head with certain profoundly radical ideas about life and their

1. A word the Communists had so successfully sullied that even its advocates had taken to using such euphemisms as "the free market." Ironically it was we, the new conservatives (and specifically my husband, in the pages of *Commentary*), who were responsible for reintroducing it in polite society.

future well-being. By the time the older ones reached adolescence, it began to dawn on me that there were marauders out there just waiting to ruin their chances of enjoying a satisfying adulthood. Those marauders were also out to bring down the country that was so generously giving them houseroom, and all around me were fine liberal people hemming and hawing and surrendering.

Put it all together, the politics and the culture, and it spelled warfare. As Jeane Kirkpatrick had signaled on that cold morning, Ronald Reagan would be the obvious political beneficiary of this warfare. So, in turn, would she. But sometimes I think that in my own peculiar way I was the one who benefited from it most of all, for I would at long last find something that sent me singing into the office every day: my very own battle station, called the Committee for the Free World.

The idea for the Committee had in a very tentative way been brewing for a couple of years. A European friend named Leopold Labedz and I would meet from time to time and say, "Why don't we . . ." —that sort of thing. Many years before there had been a big, well-heeled international organization called the Congress for Cultural Freedom, made up primarily of writers and intellectuals and artists, and dedicated to fighting off the influence of the Communists, which (as few remember) after World War II had been strong enough in Western Europe to be truly menacing. The Congress engaged in exerting cultural influence, becoming, as it were, a central clearinghouse, holding conferences and also publishing magazines in several languages. The entire enterprise came to an abrupt end when a former employee of the CIA published an article revealing that the Congress along with other groups had in fact been funded all along by the Agency through the use of certain foundations as fronts. Whereupon, overnight, the whole thing had collapsed, the unwitting Europeans rushing to profess their outrage at having been used, and the witting ones insisting, unsuccessfully, that they, too, had been ignorant about where their funding had come from.

By the late seventies, the situation in Europe was very different. Indigenous Communism was not a threat, but Soviet missiles, those ever-useful tools of political blackmail, were. And there was a new peril, this time in the United States—the peril of demoralization brought on by the seizure of national self-hatred that had spread like typhus from the sixties radicals into the major institutions of the culture. So, Leopold and I would repeatedly say, it was time to reconstitute something like the old Congress—only this time, of course, without a single penny of support from the United States government or any other.

But how to go about it? Leopold, who was a learned and brilliant man, and a tried-and-true veteran of the cultural wars against the Soviet Union, could not even find his own way to a store to buy a dozen eggs, let alone put together an organization. I had been in on the founding of the Coalition for a Democratic Majority, but all I had learned from that was a negative lesson: how *not* to bring about anything. Then one day at lunch with an acquaintance who was a longtime anti-Soviet activist among the labor unions I asked him what one must do to create a viable organization, and without blinking an eye, he said, "You must first find someone to be its executive director." "What actually does an executive director *do?*" I asked further, and he kindly and intelligently answered my question in very concrete detail. That night I tossed and turned, unable to sleep, and in the morning I sat bolt upright in my bed and said, "That's me! *I* am the executive director!"

I kissed Basic Books good-bye, after which it took three or

four months to apply for a tax exemption from the Internal Revenue Service, find an office and an assistant, and put together a board of advisers. The organization was called the Committee for the Free World, in conscious defiance of the sneer with which a large number of people in public places in those days would intone the words "the free world." I drew up a strong statement in support of both political and economic freedom and in opposition to all forces everywhere working against these freedoms, and invited primarily intellectuals, authors, academics, and scientists to sign it. If they signed, they were members; if they objected to this or that, there would be no room for them. Since we regarded ourselves as being at war, and words were to be our only weapons, we had no intention of watering down our purpose by making ourselves a large tent. In the end, we had about eight or nine thousand "members" in the United States and another thousand in the rest of the world. We knew that to begin with there would not be vast armies of us, but we thought of ourselves as being like the U.S. Cavalry in an old western fort surrounded by Indians, lighting fires and shooting off guns and moving from one side of the fort to the other to give the enemy the illusion that there were many more of us and that we were a force to be respected if not feared.

We met together just about every year at what we called a "conference" but was actually a convention whose main purpose was to keep us all in touch with one another (a very serious purpose indeed, since Committee members tended to feel isolated in their respective communities). And we put out a monthly eight-page publication, called *Contentions,* which provided analyses by four regular contributors of the nonsense or lying in articles that had appeared in newspapers or magazines or documentaries on public-affairs TV during the previous weeks. In addition to these analyses, we carried two other squib-length features without comment, one of them called "Where the Money Goes," reprinting descriptions of grants made by the major charitable foundations, and the other, called "$20,000 a Year," which simply reproduced course descriptions from the catalogues of a number of the country's major private universities. It was great fun to produce and, as people all over the place kept telling us (and tell me to this day), fun to read.

There was a certain amount of anxiety connected with all of this because it naturally required the raising of money and raising money was work at which I turned out to be, shall we say, less than brilliantly effective. The principle of taking no money from the government paid off very well, spiritually speaking (not that the government was banging down my door to give me any). For instance, as soon as we went public, the leftist magazine *The Nation* predictably rushed into print with the allegation that we were being sponsored by the CIA. So I called the editor, Victor Navasky, someone I had known in my youth, and put to him the following proposition: he could come at any time and look at my books if I could come over afterward and look at his. He never called or mentioned the subject again.

Despite my lack of great success, I learned many useful things from my stint as a fund-raiser. For one, that with only a few notable exceptions the American business community had little interest in defending the American system, probably assuming that one way or another, whoever was in power, they would find the way to get along. Of course, if you had put it that way to them, they would have objected strenuously, but, to take one example, for years only a handful of social critics recognized that many in the so-called environmental movement were actually Luddites out to do in the country's industrial might, whereas the industries most vulnerable to them appeared for a long time to believe they could be bribed with a bunch of public advertising paying obeisance to the cause of making the air and water pure once again (and very likely the industries' department of charitable giving crossed the enemy's palm with a bit of gold as well).

Another thing I learned—the hard way, I am afraid, just as the women's bank and *Ms.* magazine probably did—was that if someone of wealth is going to support you, he will do it immediately and without numerous declarations of intent. And I was lucky to have a few of these. The prospects who kept you talking and corresponding for months, on the other hand, would almost always fail to come through. The people on the Committee for the Free World's own list, however, the majority of whom were just salaried working stiffs, always came through generously when we appealed to them.

In any case, I responded to the need for money in a typically housewifely (and probably unwise) way: that is, by economizing. Our office was a sad sight indeed. It was small and by the standards of the neighborhood very cheap, in a scruffy building at a good address. For most of the time, four of us worked there, though in the last year only three. At some point our office manager out of sheer disgust bought us some rugs and drapes, but that didn't fool anyone, least of all ourselves. Once a TV crew arrived to interview me, and I could see the shock in their eyes as they tried to figure out where to place the camera. Another time the editor of a dissident Polish magazine with whom we had been in correspondence came to New York and dropped in for a visit. He, too, could not conceal his shock. *"This,"* he asked me, "this is the Free World?" I suppose I should have worked harder to raise money and put on the dog a little more, but the truth is, I was having too much fun and didn't want to take the time.

Long before this period in my life, I had suddenly begun to be invited to join this or that committee, or sit on this or that panel, by groups with whom I had never before had any contact. It was perfectly clear to me why this was happening: because as a result of feminist moral pressure, nothing of a public nature could henceforth take place without the highly visible participation of a few token women. Occasionally for some reason I would say yes to one of these invitations; mostly I would say no. In either case, the invitations most often merely made me laugh. And I couldn't understand why women would wish to be represented anywhere for so palpably corrupt a purpose, namely, to quiet the feminists' noisy demands that women be given full representation everywhere and at all times. (In my own case, there was the added fillip that since I was known to be an opponent of Women's Lib, it was no doubt assumed that I could be counted on to behave myself properly and give the men no trouble.) Surely it could not conduce to an enhancement of anyone's self-respect to be extended any kind of invitation merely for the convenience of appeasing potential troublemakers. Nor could I understand—not so much with my brain as with my nervous system—why any woman would fight for years to become a member of a club whose majority were opposed to allowing women to join. After all, affirmative action, of which my invitations were merely a foolish and glancing example, was bound to result in massive seizures of self-doubt. As it has, for instance, among some blacks in elite colleges and women learning to be fighter pilots.

Another kind of affirmative action, however, gave me great joy, and that was my being chosen to play the role of the right-wing militarist monster on a variety of TV and academic panels devoted to talking about foreign policy. In order to feel that they were being properly liberal-minded, the organizers of such discussions always felt that the hard-line position had to be represented, so they would invariably arrange that on a panel of five or six there would be one person to represent what they considered the extremist position.[2] Since some of my comrades were frightened, and others annoyed, by the thought of upholding the side all alone against a totally skewed set of opponents, I was often the one left to do the job. In fact, I usually relished doing it, for three reasons: first, because it was one of the things I was paying myself to do; second, because the smugness of my opponents tended to weaken their capacity to argue their case; and third, because being alone against many usually guaranteed a certain amount of sympathy from the audience whether or not they were in agreement. Then one day I discovered that in a certain leftist circle I had been dubbed the Dragon Lady. Could there be any greater happiness than that?

Sometimes in retrospect I ask myself, did the Committee for the Free World actually accomplish anything important along with all the pleasure we took—and, it seems, gave? I honestly don't know how to answer. By going to cultural war and taking no prisoners we seem to have made far more noise in the world than our sheer numbers would have suggested. And more important, we seem to have made a lot of people feel better and less isolated in their political attitudes.

2. Even though the majority of Americans seemed to share my view of the role America should be playing in the world, as evidenced by the large margins of both of Ronald Reagan's presidential victories, where both the press and the academics were concerned, only "extremists" would dare to hold the beliefs that were being expressed through the Committee for the Free World.

Another thing we can perhaps chalk up as an achievement of a kind was our habit of offering the use of our somewhat laughable facilities to our friends who were seeking out advice and/or help for some project that we deemed important. One of these projects was the putting together of an organization that would after a while far outstrip anything I myself had ever been able to undertake. And that is the organization of conservative academics devoted to the effort to clean out the Augean stable that is the contemporary university teaching of the liberal arts. The organization is called the National Association of Scholars. It began as a small group of distressed academics in the New York metropolitan area who, if I remember correctly, received from me the use of my mailing list, some postage, and the munificent sum of twenty-five hundred dollars with which to organize a regional conference, and who in a remarkably short time became a national force to reckon with. In my opinion that meager bit of cash was dollar for dollar among the best public-affairs monies ever spent.

In general, it seemed to me that since the Committee would never have the wherewithal to tackle every symptom of Western intellectual and cultural self-hatred, it was our responsibility to help in whatever way we could anyone who had seriously come along to join in the battle. Sometimes this meant only writing a letter or making a phone call; sometimes it meant effecting an important introduction over lunch or dinner; and now and then it meant writing a (necessarily) small check.

I would sum up the accomplishment of the Committee for the Free World as having provided a gathering place for people in a distinct political minority to feel that they were not isolated but rather the members of a cheerful if rather far-flung community, and also, with *Contentions,* to know that they had the best of the argument.

To this day I run into people who say, "Why don't you start that Committee thing up again?" For in 1990, with the collapse of the Soviet Union, I shut the organization down. It had been put together specifically to deal with a very particular set of issues, and only by faking it, I felt, could I stretch our mandate to cover the problems of the post-Soviet world.

When the Berlin Wall came down, some of us had literally wept for joy. And when the Communist regime in the Soviet Union gave way, we were beside ourselves with the kind of hope it would be difficult for anyone who had not spent his adult life keeping an eye on the evil uses of Soviet power to understand. Though freedom and democracy were a long, long way from universal, and might never be so, they seemed to me nevertheless to be *ideologically* no longer in question.

Now what we needed were two things: first, someone to clean up the mess that had been littered all over American education, from, you might say, top to bottom, and second, someone to press the president and Congress of the United States into taking responsibility for defending this country properly, from antimissile defense to a well-trained army and navy. Both of these, I thought, ought now to be turned over to younger and more muscular hands.

☙ 7 ❧

A Time to Sow,
a Time to Reap

DURING THE 1980S, something else came into my life, something far beyond the reach of, and way deeper than, politics. For beginning in March of 1980, one-two-three within the following eighteen months, my three daughters were married, and almost as rapidly began to present me with grandchildren. By the end of the decade there were in all ten of these, seven boys and three girls.

The standard line jokingly passed around among the elderly, for instance, is that grandchildren are ideal: they come over to your house, amuse you for a while, and just as the good cheer begins to wear down are conveniently whisked off home by their parents. But talking this way may in many cases merely serve as a protection from becoming mawkish. For how without sounding greeting-card inane is one to give expression to the feeling that being presented with grandchildren stirs in one? Partly it has to do with acquiring the kind of stake in the future that having children only approximates. Partly it feels like a stretching of one's identity, and thus a special expansion of one's life, beyond the day-to-day anxieties of parenthood.

Then there is that pure, sweet flesh you can revel in for the first year or so in the life of each one—before, that is, the baby struggles out of your arms and goes by one method or another to seek the world. When that happens, you discover that you will from now on be dealing with an individual will that demands to be respected, and each time another baby hits you with that discovery, it will be just as surprising. This is true of your own children as well as your grandchildren, of course, but with the latter—precisely because this time it is attended with no anxiety—each declaration of a baby's independence seems at once predictable and miraculous.

So whatever else is going on or not going on at the time, having a passel of grandchildren creeping or crawling or toddling or jumping or striding around in one's house works to sustain a continuing sense that life is among other things deeply and forever interesting.

Watching babies must bring one to another discovery, this one on the issue of what has come (illiterately) to be known as "gender." One of the earliest declarations of the feminist movement was that the social and psychological characteristics attributed respectively to males and females have been imposed by culture—and in the case of females, by culture that over the course of millennia has been aimed at oppressing and exploiting them. Some feminists, in order to put a stop to all further cultural influence of this kind, have set out to raise their children to be gender-free: little girls will be given trucks, and little boys, dolls, and so forth. Such efforts, to the extent that they were gently applied, must undoubtedly have been short-lived, the little girls having set their trucks down neatly in some corner, and the little boys having run their dolls through with the nearest available equivalent of a sword. For have you ever seen a little girl actually *play* with a truck without in some way domesticating it? And, as everyone with eyes in his head knows, a little boy deprived of toy replicas of weapons by either feminist or pacifist ideology will reach for anything at hand to serve as a gun, including, if need be, his index finger. Moreover, people who have to pay special attention to the electrical outlets in their homes, plugging up those that are not in use and perhaps, where possible, standing furniture in front of them, are for the most part the parents of boys. One simple warning, if she has noticed them at all, will usually suffice for a little girl.

In my house there is an elaborate stereo setup, consisting of twelve separate components, which takes up an entirely disproportionate amount of space in the living room. It has God knows how many different controls, buttons, switches, and blinking lights. From the moment he first begins to crawl every little boy who has ever come into that room makes a beeline for those buttons and must be told, often and firmly, not to touch them. And never has a girl, at any age, taken the slightest notice. The idea that there are no inherent differences between males and females and that such differences as seem to be evident are the imposition of a sexist culture was surely devised by someone who had never been in the presence of children for more than twenty seconds.

As the years of experiencing grandparenthood move along, you lose the sensation of mere wonderment at the power of your connection to these babies, and they become people you get to know better and better. In my own case there are no two grandchildren even faintly alike (including the two youngest, who are fraternal twins, one of each sex): this one too clever by half, that one preternaturally sensitive, another a determined little striver, the fourth, like his maternal uncle, smitten with the stage, and so on. Taken all together they have been for me an unending source of fascination.

When they were babies, year by year, I was a fairly active attendant grandmother—even, every so often, with the four who live in Jerusalem. But now that they are quite grown, some in college, some soon to be in college, one in the Israeli army, one in the U.S. Navy, and even the youngest not so far from entering junior high school, I am no longer much needed as a baby-sitter and our relations with one another have become quite different. When I turn up on their doorsteps, or, as is more likely, when they turn up on mine, they are all reasonably friendly and even very affectionate, but they are also, as they should be, almost totally preoccupied with the lives they lead beyond the circle of family. Through it all I have remained part of the furniture of their lives, around in the background in case of need.

So for most of the time I am a watcher from the sidelines, hoping that one way and another I am tipping them off to the fact that I still keep a close eye on them, and leaving all shows of worry and concern about them to their parents. Some day— who knows?—I might now and then on that account even be of some genuine use to them. Meanwhile, before, and after, everything else, they fill my thoughts. To this day, I cannot get over their existence.

In the world of early feminist-speak, one is hard put to find mention of grandchildren. Or, in fact, of grandmothers either. "Mature"—or what in bygone days was referred to as "elderly"—women are the objects of attention only insofar as they are either admirable for continuing the fight for their rights or deserving of special support in a society that refuses to find the cure for such diseases as breast or uterine cancer. Yet most of the women I know who have reached their late fifties and beyond long for grandchildren if they do not have them or feel blessed if they do. Perhaps they have admired, and even envied, their daughters who set out to make their way in the world before settling down to marry and have a family. But as the years go by I have watched them growing fearful that their admirable, and even enviable, daughters may contrive to leave them untied to a second generation.

I know many such women, the ones filled with the longing I have described: we have gone to school together, worked together, dined together, and even on occasion ideologically duked it out with one another. For the most part, the women I am talking about were once ardently in favor of the new ordering of young women's lives and regarded my opposition to the women's movement as puzzling or criminal or both. When I would argue that the movement was not some kind of trade union seeking equal pay and better working conditions for women, that on the contrary, it was seeking to create a breach in women's very nature, they would hoot or grow red in the face with anger. After a while, it simply became impossible for us to talk about the subject. But as the years went by, these acquaintances of mine—who were very far from alone among the members of their generation—became ever more audibly anxious: why didn't their daughters marry? Why did they spend so many years living with this man or that without finding someone with whom they wished to settle down? And, would there ever be grandchildren?

I would occasionally receive a wedding announcement from those daughters, but the birth announcements were few and far between. And then quite suddenly, as if Mother Nature had slammed down her fist in annoyance, there came the announcement of a great race against what the no-longer-quite-so-young women called the biological clock. One could weep for all those young women who were so immersed in the issue of their fair share of the world's goodies that for years the likelihood that they would want to have a baby or two had somehow been tucked away for some vague and abstract future. Was it now too late?

For some perhaps it was; for others the rush was on for fair. Those who happened to be married convinced their husbands (who may have needed little or no convincing). And those who were unmarried set about quickly to remedy the shortcoming. And soon the longing of many of my contemporaries to see a new generation, even among those who had not verbally owned up to it, was to be requited.

That was what you might call stage one—what the demographers dubbed the baby boomlet. Partly the reason for its being a "boomlet" is that in order to create a real boom, you have to start very young, as we did after World War II. The boomlet babies were to a great extent the result of a realization—the old clock ticking away—that it was now, or at least soon, or never. In any case, especially in those neighborhoods in which the high-achieving baby boomers tended to congregate, the once quiet and stately streets began to be filled with baby strollers—for the most part, to be sure, being pushed by Jamaican or Dominican or Filipina nannies.

After she married and in quick order produced two little boys, my number two daughter lived for a time just down the street from me. Each day she would take the toddlers to play—which at their age basically meant jumping around a lot to expend a little of their explosive energy—in a nearby park. There she sat each afternoon on a bench opposite the sandbox or slide with not a soul to talk to. The nannies had their own tight and exclusive little society, and no other mother was in sight. (Sometimes of a Saturday it would be the child's mother who accompanied him to the park, and as my daughter described for us, on such occasions a mother could be quite at sea, inquiring, should the child set out to do something a bit daring, "Does Maria allow you to do that?")

As it happened, after a time my daughter would be released from her park-time penance by moving to Washington, where she could hang out with her older sister, who happened also to be her best friend. But her time on that park bench had left its mark on her sense of the world. Not long after she had settled in Washington, she had a third child, this time a little girl, and there was a period when I would jokingly say of that grand-daughter that she would be lucky if her mother some day let her out of her arms long enough for her to go to school.

The baby boomlet may never have become a proper boom, but it has gone through a very important second stage. "Stage" is perhaps not the right word: for many of the women who to begin with found within themselves a deep longing to have a baby that their feminist mentors and guides had neglected to tell them about soon made a second, and even more startling, discovery. They had certainly endorsed the movement's de-mand that the government enact a guarantee of three months' maternity leave for every working woman who gave birth to a new baby;[1] but lo and behold . . . to their astonishment many of these new mothers discovered that after three months they were not necessarily enthusiastic about the prospect of leaving this new creature in other hands and returning to work. And soon one would begin to see ever greater numbers of

---

1. Or to her husband, if it should be determined that he was to be the baby's primary "caregiver."

fashionable, well-heeled, not-quite-so-young women marching along the sidewalks of prosperous New York behind a veritable fleet of baby strollers.

That astonishment at the discovery of unforeseen maternal
passion would turn out to be a very heavy nail in the coffin of
ideological feminism. For the women who were astonished in
this way might continue, say, to vote like feminists, or even
now and then make feminist gestures at dinner parties, but the
one or two small passengers being moved through the streets
by her in their child conveyance know better. They know, for
instance, that whatever she might say in the abstract, when
push comes to shove it is really they who hold the ultimate
power in the relations between them. She may have been a pis-
tol in the boardroom or courtroom, but her baby's tears leave
her helpless (often helplessly angry, but helpless all the same).

One day in early March 2000, the New York Times carried a
story about the latest new development in Hollywood: the
presence on the scene of a woman they call the "baby whis-
perer" (after the movie in which a character played by Robert
Redford cures terrified or deranged horses by magically whispering to them). It seems that she makes house calls to the
homes of the stars—for which she naturally receives extrava-
gant sums of money—and quiets their high-strung and unhappy babies by, among other techniques, walking around with
the babies fit snugly on her shoulder, rhythmically stroking
their backs, and whispering magical sounds into their ears.
"She is unbelievable," her clients all attest; they don't know
what it is she does, or how exactly she does it, but after a few
sessions with her their offspring are calm and cheerful!

This story ought to leave one laughing: walking the floor
with the baby, patting its back and crooning into its ear—who
but a high-paid Hollywood wizard could have thought of

doing such things to soothe an unhappy or uncomfortable baby? But it doesn't somehow seem funny. Not even though it is about Hollywood, where simple ordinary impulses must be in short supply with respect to many kinds of relations besides those with one's babies. It isn't funny because the amount of space devoted to it in the *Times* suggests that the paper's editors must have felt the story would be of interest to the paper's readers far beyond mere gossip about the doings of the rich and famous. And it seems they may be right: whatever they say about the matter, editors of newspapers and magazines usually edit in accordance with their own interests (when they say "our readers," more often than not they mean themselves). The reason the editor, or editors, might have found this story to be worth more space and attention than the kind of brief squib that many papers reserve for some casual oddity is that, as in Hollywood, the achieving not-so-young mothers who read the *Times* have never spent enough time even in the vicinity of so mysterious a being as a baby to know about the nigh-universal techniques of walking, patting, and crooning. Those of us who were responsible for producing the postwar, i.e., the original, baby boom had also known nothing about the care of babies— in our case, not because we had been too busy training for a serious career but because, being children of the Depression, most of us, at least most of us non-Catholics, had grown up in very small families and thus had virtually no experience of the tiny creatures. The difference was that there were so many of us new mothers hanging out together—wherever we lived— and so many babies lying around or crawling around underfoot, we simply could not remain strangers to the process for long. And, remember, we were younger and hence a little steadier of nerve or at least more naturally energetic than these new mothers, who tended to come to the vocation rather late in life and for whom mothering was undoubtedly being experienced at first as an isolated—and isolating—experience.

In the earlier stage of the "boomlet," when such a thing as a young affluent mother was not to be seen in or near her home from sunup to sundown, I have many times watched—in the supermarket, say, or on a street corner where two or more "nannies" were hanging out chatting together—a woman stand with her back turned to some miserable crying toddler and give not the slightest indication that she has even heard him, let alone that she might at any time soon acknowledge his distress. This stand-off can go on for as long as half an hour. She does not attempt to comfort or cajole him, nor does she scold him— she simply does not hear him. I used to wonder, do these babies' mothers have any idea of what happens to their little ones when they are not around?

Nowadays there is little cause for such wondering, because if it is not the baby's mother one is most likely to see him with, it is his grandmother, come to relieve her daughter or daughter-in-law for an afternoon's recreation. (This, alas, was not something I could do for my own daughters, for to see to their children in any way meant my coming to visit for a while, especially in the case of the one in Israel but also in Washington, where the rest of them live: it had to be planned and could not simply be over at the end of a day or evening.) A grandmother might not be physically up to the task of making the child's life as interesting as it is when he is in the care of his mother. I often run into one of these grandmothers—in the lobby of my apartment building, for instance—and sharing an elderly moment with me, they will sigh and smilingly say something about being worn out by the end of the day. The child, on the other hand, while perhaps he has not been what the experts like to refer to as "stimulated," is quite at peace. He is under the watchful eye of someone who would kill for him, and don't think for a moment that he doesn't know it.

Beyond the shock of discovering the power of their maternal instinct, many mothers of little ones are beginning to understand what neither the women's movement nor their feminist professors ever mentioned to them—and what my own daughters have lately come to provide a most persuasive example of—and that is, that there is time for everything in this long and healthy life: time to devote to one's children and time in the years after that to find a satisfying career, if such is what they should one day want to do.

Simple as it sounds when it is put that way, this is not an easy thought to come by. Career has been so much at the center of young women's self-respect; arriving at the decision to take a chance on life at home might leave them with the fear that they are about to disappear from the face of the earth. Or at least that in their absence all their colleagues will have gone roaring ahead, leaving them far behind in the race they will undoubtedly wish to take up later. And chances are that neither their friends nor the larger social community in which they have been living nor the culture in general will be of any real help in reassuring them.

Some years ago I took part in a panel discussion about the ostensible plight of women in journalism. This panel, in keeping with the general state of affairs in those days, was made up almost completely of women complaining that they were not being given the really prestigious jobs on their newspapers. Also present was Anna Quindlen, a famous and highly successful author and columnist, whom they began to berate because she had been offered a high editorial job on the *New York Times* and turned it down to go home, look after her kids, and be a writer. She had let down the side, they complained; as a successful journalist she had owed it to her feminist sisters to take the big job at the *Times* and blaze the trail for others. They were going at her hot and heavy, whereupon no doubt to her amazement (for I was, and am, not among the greatest admirers of the lady's work) I broke into the discussion to defend her. "She can be at home with her kids now," I argued, "and later on if she should want to, she could come back to the *Times* or anywhere else." This produced a howl of derision: did I really think that you could leave a good job and then just come back to it? Where do you think they would put her by then? In the mail room? And so on. At this point a handsome and elegantly dressed middle-aged woman, who had sat through the entire panel discussion without saying a word, intervened. She is right, she said, pointing to me. As it happens, I did just that—I left my job to raise my children and when they were grown, I went back to work again. "Who is that?" I whispered to the man who was serving as the moderator. "She?" he said. "Why, she is the editor in chief of a very important southern newspaper. In fact, she is the highest-ranking working woman in the American newspaper business today." I said to myself, "God really loves me today."

For usually I played the role of the lone dissenter on such panels, and ended with the feeling that it was hopeless to try to talk even a little bit seriously in the company of these immovable party-liners. They were after all not really interested in women or the experiences of women; what they really wanted (aside from the promotions that putting pressure on their employers might bring them) was to impose on the world their definition of reality. And the men who sat by nodding sympathetically at their complaints would do what they have always done in the face of feminist assault: they would smile and turn off their hearing aids.

Be that as it may, we may be looking at what will turn out to be a new pattern of women's employment, namely, education first, then children, and then career. All the women who fear, as those panelists claimed to do, that time taken out will be time lost forever either fail or refuse to understand that the seasoning gained from the experiences of motherhood might one day prove to be of great professional value, both to them and to their employer. Two of my daughters, perhaps without even knowing it, have discovered this. (One is a public relations executive, one a newspaper editor, and the third works in her own basement as a professional ceramist, and even she has a far greater sense of assurance about what she is doing than she could ever have had twenty years earlier.) Training is naturally a help to someone who is in the process of assuming a serious kind of authority. But ask any intelligent boss and he or she will tell you that when it comes to employing someone, her being emotionally and spiritually a grown-up is a far greater asset than mere training.

Another decade has gone by since those first startling and heavenly days of my grandmotherhood, and there they are: my daughters no longer playmates of their children and no longer nearly so much engaged in their practical care, and my grandchildren, except for the three youngest, struggling to break free. (And the time of those three will be coming along soon.) And they are, though more distant, in a way also far more interesting to me. But I miss the touch of baby flesh, and I believe that most women who have ever had a taste of it also come to miss it when it is gone. Watch people looking through the wide glass window of a maternity nursery. There are the new parents, staring intently at this strange-looking little creature who is about to become the dictator of their lives; they are moved and tense in equal parts. Then there are the grandparents (grandmothers especially because as a rule grandfathers, being men, tend to be made nervous by the sheer delicacy of newborns). Unconsciously their hands tend to stroke the glass, as if they might go through and caress all those newborn creatures.

My son, who is undoubtedly the world's greatest uncle, has as of this writing not yet become a father. So there may be hope of finding another little creature wiggling on our carpet some day. Meanwhile I pester the babies of our young neighbors. And I notice that I am not the only mature woman in our building to do so.

❧8❧

Happy Days
Were Here Again

NOR WERE MY PLEASURES in the 1980s restricted to those spent raising hell with the world in the office of the Committee for the Free World and savoring the fascinations of grandchildren. There were new friendships and new things to think about and there was the discovery of Washington, D.C.—not only the place where by the end of the decade three of my four children had settled themselves, but a place of passions that were entirely new and fascinating to me.

Washington in the eighties was, of course, Ronald Reagan's Washington. For some neoconservatives like me it was the first time in our lives that we felt truly welcomed, and truly close to the political action. Our politics until that moment in history had been mainly theoretical, that is, carried on in argument above the day-to-day fray—even in the case of my feeble effort to help save the Democratic party from the leftists by signing on to the Coalition for a Democratic Majority. But now I found myself throwing my whole heart into just about every aspect of the battle that Reagan as candidate had called us to— from restoring the love of country, to fighting Castro in Cuba, to overthrowing the current regime in Nicaragua, to cutting taxes, to bringing down the Soviet Union, to engaging in the search for a system of missile defense. Nothing in this agenda would in essence have been new to me—except perhaps for missile defense, which in those days loomed as an entirely new possibility—but that the *president of the United States* was asking us to join him in making it national policy . . . ! Bliss it was to be alive at that hour—and, even if one was no longer young, very heaven.

In his memoir of the Kennedy administration Arthur Schlesinger speaks most evocatively of the new glitter that had been splattered across dreary Washington when John F. Kennedy came to the White House. And after Kennedy's assassination, a young assistant secretary of Labor named Daniel Patrick Moynihan remarked to an interviewer, "All our revels are now ended." It is easy for me to understand how they felt, for though the Kennedy administration in the brevity of its tenure left little behind that was memorable (aside, that is, from America's involvement in the Vietnam War), it clearly gave a crew of young and young-at-heart intellectuals the sense that their stodgy old country had now fully recovered from the constraints of World War II and its aftermath and was now theirs to make new. And I can understand as well how it is that until this day many of the old denizens of Camelot speak of that brief moment with nostalgia. For however short a time, Washington was their oyster, and, as I was discovering, there is no experience quite like it.

As it happened, glitter was not what we were after, we

Reaganites—quite the opposite. We were looking to restore something solid and permanent that seemed to have been lost with the longing for Camelot and all that came after it. Call what we were about, for the sake of brevity, hatred of collectivism (most especially Soviet Communism), simple love of country, and republican (small "r") virtue. And there was Ronald Reagan, announcing his determination to be an agent for the restoration of exactly all that. He did not, could not, succeed, of course; nor, I suppose, could or should we really have expected him to. But at least the fight was on, and at least, mirabile dictu, the power was with us. Suddenly our views seemed deeply interesting to the journalists, most of whom had been puzzled about what they saw as the sudden and inexplicable upsurge of conservatism. (A classic, though somewhat earlier, case of the bewilderment of the press with respect to conservatism was that of Pauline Kael, doyenne of American film critics, who in late 1972 famously said, "I simply can't believe that Richard Nixon won this election by a landslide. I don't know a *single person* who voted for him.")

The "we" of which I have been speaking here was made up of what would once surely have seemed to the naked eye an odd cast of characters to be acting together in the same drama: the old Goldwater insurgents from 1964, dreaming of finding another, and perhaps truer, champion; businessmen longing to throw off the shackles of regulation; Christian conservatives new to politics who had grown bitter about the insults to their faith so tightly woven into the fabric of public education as well as the arts; and neoconservatives out to fight Communism abroad and affirmative action and the debasement of culture at home.

To begin with, the various elements in this coalition eyed one another with the deepest suspicion, and truth to tell, may never have come to hold one another in a simple brotherly embrace. But there would prove to be enough common opposition to things as they were to keep them all pretty much together and sometimes even bring them quite close, politically if not culturally speaking.

For me, however, an odd, and as it would turn out unbelievably happy, circumstance would carry me comfortably beyond all such tensions: put me squarely in the heart of Reagan Washington, induce me to drop the prefix "neo" from my conservatism, and above all, provide me with lifelong alliances as well as some deep friendships. I am referring to my relation to a conservative Washington think tank called the Heritage Foundation.

The original purpose of the Heritage Foundation had been to educate and influence legislators—members of the Senate and House of Representatives and their staffs—about the veritable cataract of legislation that poured down upon their desks each day for them to make up their minds about. Such a purpose was by its very nature bound to require being expanded upon, because legislation, whether good or bad, does not after all emerge full-blown from the brow of Zeus but arises from the motion of the tectonic plates beneath the culture. So the foundation's research had early on begun to widen beyond legislation and even beyond legislative policies and to touch on what lay beneath them.

As a kind of foretelling of Reagan's Washington, one day in the late seventies my husband and I answered an invitation to come to Heritage and lecture, he at lunch and I in the evening. I don't remember what I spoke about; the subject was probably Women's Lib, because I could not remember when I had had such a pleasant, friendly audience. Not long after that, out of the blue, as it were, Ed Feulner, the president of Heritage, invited me to lunch. To my astonishment he asked me if I would be willing to serve on his board of trustees, and perhaps somewhat to his astonishment I took no more than three seconds to say yes. I hadn't the faintest idea what a trustee of the Heritage Foundation was expected to be, or do, but I heard a voice speaking the sentence "You must always join the side you're on," and the voice I heard was my own.

I would remember that sentence in the years ahead, as I began to occupy myself with the Committee for the Free World and encountered people whose views I knew to be at least as anti-Communist and opposed to leftist culture as mine but who hemmed and hawed about taking a so much frowned-upon position in public. "It's okay," I wrote to one of these, "you may remain comfortable in your superior position, like France, and like the United States, we will nevertheless be happy to offer you the protection of our nuclear umbrella."

I understood that as far as the old conservative activists were concerned I was not much more than an "affirmative action baby," but to begin with, I wasn't sure which quota I was supposed to be filling. Those were the days when just about every board in the land included one woman, but I didn't believe that covering the Heritage Foundation's backside on that score could have been what the board and Feulner had in mind. Was I perhaps there as a Jew? I very much doubted it. It must have been that I had been invited as a representative of that weird new ex-liberal breed from New York City who had somehow popped up to lend their words and publications to the conservative movement. In other words, the neocons. Indeed, when I asked Ed Feulner the question a couple of years later, he said that he had "wanted to make a statement"—a statement about the conservative community being, as the politicos say, a big tent. The problem was that I could hardly be of service in enlarging the conservative tent because every time I met one of the leaders of the old-time conservatism, I discovered that we were in total agreement about everything that mattered. The would-be ambassador from neoconservativeland turned out no longer to be a citizen in good standing of that bright young country.

One very special contribution that the neocons in particular were making to the conservative enterprise, however, was the result of our far superior knowledge of the country's true enemies, particularly its leftist enemies at home. Unlike the old conservatives, we had known the leftists very intimately: we had been reading their books and magazines for years; we had spent a good deal of energy arguing with them; some of us had *been* them. Thus we knew where their nerves were most exposed and their hypocrisy most naked. All of which meant that we knew how most effectively to conduct polemics against them. This gave us a certain special value to Reagan as well as to the conservative movement in general.

So it was that many people I knew, and even members of my own family—two sons-in-law and for a brief time near the end of Reagan's second term, my son—worked for the Reagan administration.[1] For the first time, which was the last time, in my own life the United States government was up close and personal. Indeed, I myself had been invited to serve on both a presidential commission and the board of Radio Broadcasting to Cuba, a propaganda enterprise consisting mainly of a radio

1. Though one of these sons-in-law, Elliott Abrams, Assistant Secretary of State for Inter-American Affairs, as the result of a monstrous injustice would one day pay a heavy price for having loyally carried out Reagan's policy in Central America.

station called Radio Marti. The commission was nothing, really, basically a technique for shutting up a hostile press, and we produced a study that no one read. And oddly enough, my basic value to Radio Marti, since I had no Spanish, was the fact that I was still a registered Democrat. Being a government enterprise, Radio Marti needed to have board representation from both parties—and how convenient that the Democrat should have been little old hotheaded Midge. (I have subsequently served this role on other projects as well, and thus have never changed my party affiliation.)

I was now also faithfully included among the conservative group who were occasionally invited to meet with the president. Each time we prepared our agenda carefully, one person to an issue, and the president listened most politely. But I had learned from the chilling experience of meeting with Jimmy Carter that you ought not to come to the president of the United States with a whole assortment of agenda items: to be taken truly seriously, a delegation must arrive with one thing only on its mind. Our meetings with Reagan, in any case, were mainly ritual occasions on which he was extending a special courtesy to a group who he understood were among his most ardent loyalists.

It was on one of these occasions that I witnessed what was to me a truly shocking scene. Before our meeting commenced, just as we had all taken our places around the table and the president had arrived to take his, a group of men with cameras filed by from one end of the room to the other snapping pictures. And as they filed by, several of them shouted rude questions at Reagan: "What have you got up your little sleeve now, Mr. President?" and "Are you lying to the American people, Mr. President?" All the while this was taking place, Reagan remained completely impassive. "What the hell is going on?" I whispered to Pat Buchanan,[2] who happened to be sitting next to me. "This," said Pat, "is what they call a photo op." "You mean," I asked, "that this is allowed to go on all the time?"—to which Pat shrugged and nodded. To this day I cannot get over what I witnessed that day.

Unlike many people I knew, and high-hearted as I felt during most of the Reagan years, I was never for one second infected with the malady they call Potomac Fever. If working for the government does not succeed in depressing you with its constant demand for circumspection, it will soon find the means for punishing you for having too good a time. Somehow the ground beneath your feet is never entirely solid. (And as for elective office, what could be a more exacting and exhausting grind?) Meanwhile, there I was, in my dark and smoky little office in New York, having the time of my life.

Of all the Washington figures whom I came to know well in those years there is no one who is quite so unlikely a character as Ed Feulner. For he was an entirely singular combination of high-mindedness, innocent generosity, and street smarts. Like me, he is a Middle Westerner, but unlike me and most of our breed, he neither rebels against—nor defines himself by—that circumstance. Since the day I joined the board (and alas, no thanks to me), Heritage has prospered mightily. It has in fact become a permanent, major Washington institution, with a large staff, a huge budget, and its fingers in many different pies. Instructing Congress and, when possible, the White House, is still the bottom line of its activities, but it has stretched itself far

2. This was the Pat Buchanan who was our most valuable comrade-in-arms and had not yet become a most unpleasant and unacceptable kind of nativist.

beyond that. Ed presides over it all, with assistance in managing the day-to-day operations from another deceptively clever, this time soft-spoken, southern gentleman named (as if he were a character in a morality play) Phil Truluck.

Because of Ed's innocence he has more than once been "put on" in a serious way, but on the other hand, he has astutely managed to remain the honest broker among the various inevitably competing conservative activists. You can warn him that someone near him is a sly sonofabitch—the sort of second sight that we ex-liberals seems to come specially equipped with—but until he actually feels the knife in his back, he keeps his mind open. You would think that this is a far from useful characteristic in a place like Washington, and almost certainly you would be right, but not, it seems, in this one case. Nor in twenty years have I ever seen him put his feet up and remark that he is tired.

Between the Committee for the Free World and the Heritage Foundation, I felt it was probably sinful to have such a good time as I was having and simultaneously make a reasonable living doing it. In addition to the everyday managerial details that crossed my desk, I was doing some occasional magazine writing, putting out my eight-page *Contentions,* and spending a good deal of time on the hustings. I woke up each day feeling more energetic than the day before.

A major preoccupation of all of us in those days was Central America. Truth to tell, this was a region of the world to which, except for the academic experts, few Americans had ever paid much attention. Probably the same thing could be said of the whole of Latin America, despite the claim of presidents all the way from James Monroe on that we had a vital interest there. But because of Fidel Castro, Cuba, once a happy playground for gamblers and sunbathers, had indeed become vitally interesting to everybody. Castro himself and his right-hand man Che Guevara had since their revolution triumphed in 1959 been taken for the kind of romantic revolutionary heroes that leftist lady newspapermen dreamed of sleeping with, and that the men of the radical movement longed to emulate. And because Castro's Cuba had become essentially a satellite of the Soviet Union, for the antiradicals among us Communism was coming too close to home to be tolerated. So people like me and the rest of the members of the Committee for the Free World found ourselves first becoming passionate about a leftist insurgency in El Salvador, which was more or less effectively being held off by the democratically elected government of the place, and then even more seriously preoccupied with the successful takeover of Nicaragua by a Communist-dominated coalition called the Sandinistas. In this latter case, the insurgency was on the other foot, that is, a peasant army called the Contras were fighting (as it would turn out, with a fair amount of success) to overturn the newly installed Sandinista regime. And however far-off and unknown to most Americans these insurgencies had been to begin with, it would not be long before the Reagan administration, along with the Congress and the whole of the academic-intellectual community in America, would be embroiled with them.

The question essentially boiled down to this: was the government of the United States going to oppose the spread of Communism into our very own neighborhood or not? In the case of Castro we had failed—in fact had been unwilling—to do so. And I remember attending a lecture by the American ambassador to Nicaragua around the beginning of the Sandinistas' move on Managua, in which he was explaining that the Sandinistas were no more than a coalition of various democratic forces. In other words, he was advising his government that there was no need to take action. I, who was after all no expert, could not believe my ears: after all this time did this American ambassador not know how the Communists operated?[3] But now it was Ronald Reagan who sat in the White House, so the advance of Communism would not be allowed to stand.

And in its own small but noisy and joyous way the Committee for the Free World mounted a campaign to support the administration in Central America. For this we lost certain of our members from the labor movement. Indeed, with each campaign we mounted this individual or that would write me a letter announcing that he was dropping out of our effort. This happened rather notably in the case of one stunt of ours concerning the present-day corruption of what a wag my husband and I once knew called "the quality lit biz." That is, in *Contentions* we rereviewed the books that had won Pulitzer Prizes for that year and opposed our judgments to those of the Pulitzer board. This might have sounded like nothing to get heated up about, but Saul Bellow resigned because of it, on the ground that opposing Communism was one thing but why were we mucking around in the literary culture? So it was that we lost one of our major celebrities. But we didn't really mind his resignation, for the literary culture happened to be key to what we were fighting against; moreover, circumspection is not a quality helpful for carrying on an ideological war. (In those days I used to remind myself regularly of something said to one of his classes by a friend who was teaching political philosophy

---

3. Later I read that this gentleman had been taken hostage by some revolutionary group while he was attending a dinner party, and I must confess that a rather nasty wave of schadenfreude broke over me. Fortunately he was quickly released, or I might never have recovered from my feeling of guilt at the pleasure I took in his having been administered such an effective punishment for his stupidity.

at Cornell. Once at the end of class a student came to him and protested that his lecture that day had not included any other point of view but his own. "Madam," he replied, "I am not the National Broadcasting Corporation.")

But of course our major preoccupation through the years was the Soviet Union. Not that we had either the intention or the wherewithal to influence the United States Departments of State and Defense—which were in any case doing just fine at that particular moment—nor the White House, which aside from the fatal mistake of not confronting Congress head-on when it came to Nicaragua, was making us happy as well.

Thus our targets were focused mainly on the press and the intellectual community, which for years had in essence been maintaining either that the Soviet Union was too strong for us to mess with or too weak for us to have to bother with—and sometimes both at the same time.

One day in 1982, it may be remembered, Reagan happened to refer to the Soviet Union as "the evil empire." He was saying something he undoubtedly meant, but doing so with a certain dash of flippancy. For those who no longer remember, be it said that the press went positively ape. You would have thought that the missiles would be flying any minute now. And not until the Soviets collapsed in 1990 were many Russians, especially those still in the Gulag, able to explain to Western acquaintances how that remark had struck them. They had heard no lesser a personage than the president of the United States *himself* openly call the murderers and thugs who had been oppressing them for more than sixty years "evil"! The most powerful man in the world out there knew what they had been going through and *cared*! At home the press attacked him and called him dangerously careless of tongue and light-minded for having said such a thing to the world at large. But there in the

Soviet Union he had lifted everyone's spirits. (It is a curious thing about the press. They make a living with words, and yet at least half of the time hope—and possibly even believe—that words don't really count for much. Whereas, of course, for those with ears to hear they sometimes count for everything.)

I met Reagan three or four times. And each time I met him he always gave the impression of being cordially attentive. Naturally he never recognized me—on every occasion I was introduced anew—and I doubt he recognized many of the rest of us either. He was indeed, as by all accounts he was touted to be, perpetually amiable and pleasant. Which means that he must at the core have been a very cold man, for after all only someone whose heart is very distant from the people and day-to-day proceedings all around him can remain perpetually pleasant. And at the end of eight years when he left Washington, he blithely left behind him, clearly without giving it another moment's thought, a group of public servants who were in deep trouble for doing nothing worse than loyally carrying out his policy.

In Reagan's second term, my son, too, was working for the president—and up close, for he had become a presidential speechwriter. He appeared to be having quite a marvelous time, and the addition of speechwriting to his already rather mixed bag of journalistic experience suited him well, at least for the time he was engaged in it. He was given an office that seemed to me to be bigger than Grand Central Station, and being in the White House—particularly with his wicked eye— surely taught him things about the way the world works he might never have learned in a lifetime of ordinary journalism.

Two years after Reagan left office, the Soviet government collapsed, leaving in its wake a struggling and beset, but hopeful, facsimile of democracy. Washington was no longer quite so entertaining, and far less had been accomplished, far less change brought about, than we conservatives had anticipated; but for millions of people in Eastern Europe the world had become a decisively better place. That was something to celebrate, though no actual celebration would take place for many years: for we were at that moment too caught up in our own local political and cultural battles.

Anyway, conservatives seem to have a hard time taking yes for an answer.

The Reagan days were also a very good time in my private life. During most of that decade I was in my fifties, and it seems to me that, providing she is healthy, the fifties can be particularly good years in a woman's life. For by that age she has safely passed through the whole process of becoming: who and what she is going to be, she is.

American culture is constantly pressuring people, especially, it seems to me, women, to make themselves new: to buy themselves new faces, to reengineer their bodies, to take on new regimens and new forms of recreation, to refashion their minds, to discover new and uncharted territories in their psyches. Much of this pressure is commercial, of course, but commercial or not, it demands of people—again, especially women—to live in a continuing state of anxious hope. But even with a thoroughly lifted and uplifted face, a woman of, say, fifty-five is far more apt to know exactly who and what she is than to mistake herself for the maiden she now resembles. For while her skin and muscles may have grown newly supple, her desires and capacities have narrowed and have been both toughened and enriched thereby.

What some people do not understand, no doubt because it

goes against what they are being told night and day, is that there is great comfort in sloughing off youthful possibilities. When I was in my late twenties, for instance, and had just divorced my first husband, I was so restless and full of disgust with the two of us that had I stuck around I might at some point have pushed one or both of us from a high window. With my second husband I was at peace from the first moment. At peace with him, that is; with myself it would take a very long time. Indeed, not until I reached my fifties—not yet old but, thank God, no longer anywhere near young—that I could say with confidence, "Well, kid, this is it, this is who you are. Make the best of it." Perhaps becoming a grandmother had something to do with this new acceptance. Or perhaps it was the way my husband refused, when he encountered it, to be much impressed with my dark side. Once or twice it even made him laugh.

Oh, that saving laughter.

Even a middle-aged woman who has been most bitterly betrayed—that is, when she has seen her husband through to the point of great success and he, seized by the fear of growing old, dumps her for a handsome young "trophy wife"—will almost certainly find the means to make a new life for herself. Bitter she may properly be, but neither helpless nor hopeless. The reason for this is that she has cast away all girlish illusion and, whether she wills it or not, is at least to some extent and one way or another in fighting trim.

About one thing, however, I did not—and to this day do not—say "This is it," and that is the color of my hair. It has been many different shades and hues, my hair, from my fifties until now. Nor was the source of this last bit of will to hang on to something resembling youth at all a mystery to me. For my mother, who died at the age of seventy-eight, was one of those women grown old way before their time. In her fifties she already looked like—and dressed and carried herself like—an elderly woman and, despite the fact that she was both a communal and family powerhouse, she moved like an elderly woman as well. I don't know why. Perhaps it was that while she was the youngest of her siblings, very early on she had taken the role of the only real grown-up among them. Or perhaps it was genes: her hair, for example, had turned very gray when she was only in her forties. On the other hand, my oldest sister had inherited from her the tendency to turn gray very young, and she never seemed old because of it. Nor did my father, who stayed vigorous well into his eighties. For many years, as I said, my mother used to work with my father in his business. One day a customer came into the place and began to look around, and when my mother asked him if she could be of help, he said, referring to my father, "I'd like to speak to your son." This story became part of family lore, and my mother, who can't have been pleased by it, was nevertheless much too sunk in virtue to complain at its frequent repetition. In any case, the point is that for one reason or another she spent some part of what should have been no more than middle age sinking into old womanhood. She continued to be able to do a hundred things at once, but my two younger children remember that they never heard her laugh. Thus I vowed long ago that I would hang on to this one purely symbolic mark of vigor—grayless hair—with the continuing aid of my trusty hairdresser.

But hair aside, through most of the Reagan decade I was in my fifties, still young but no longer "young," still with a full supply of energy but no longer troubled by the question of what was to become of me. What could be better than that? As I write, my two elder daughters are approaching their fifties. I once told them that being in your forties was much better than being in your thirties—so much youthful turmoil abated—and I suspect that by now they have probably come to agree with me. But soon they will find themselves in a time of life even better than that.

Many of the mothers of the baby boomlet are starting out in their new maternal estate already having reached their forties. They are the ones who spent their young womanhood, willingly or not, under the aegis of the women's movement: being taught that their careers comprise the true freedom and equality; being taught that a woman cannot, or at any rate should not, place her fate entirely in the hands of some man; being admonished to preserve for themselves something called their own "space"; and, more often than not, at least being whispered to if not shouted at that husbands are a drag and children are a drain. Thus they have had to learn very late how to listen to the call of their own hearts. They will almost certainly miss the pleasures I have been describing, for when they are in their fifties, their lives will still be in the thick of youthful things even though their bodies may be asking for something else.

9

Last Things, and First

WHEN THE NINETIES came along, we conservatives lost two things that had been key to the organization of our energies. Ronald Reagan, as all good presidents must, sailed off into the sunset and soon afterward the Soviet Union lost its grip and surrendered to the pull of a whole array of different forces, both centrifugal and centripetal. As it happened, my husband and I had gone to Moscow in 1987 at a time when the cracks in the system were beginning to show daylight, and we could see them, though we did not fully understand what we were looking at. Mikhail Gorbachev, as we knew, had embarked on an effort to keep the Soviet government together by loosening some of its restrictiveness. Perestroika may have been a clever policy, but turned out to be too little too late—though neither he, nor of course we, understood that yet. Even though hard-bitten anti-Communists like us were in Moscow being treated royally as guests of the Soviet government in order to take part with a group of other Americans in a weeklong public seminar on democracy, we did not see how close to the end of Communist rule we were.

Our Russian audience was large, made up mostly of academics, and remained consistently so throughout the week. It had been arranged that each of us was to give a speech on the subject of Western democracy, and when my turn came, I was timid and uncomfortable: imagine lecturing in, of all places, Moscow, where I had never been before and thus had only an abstract sense of the intellectual terrain. So I had carefully written out my talk—alluding to Tolstoy and Solzhenitsyn, that sort of thing—and when during the question period one of my questioners praised my "elegance," I knew I had blown it. My husband, however, took hold of the opportunity with both hands and delivered a stern analysis of how and why the Soviet Union was solely responsible for the Cold War. The audience was deeply stirred, whether to rage or fascination it was at first difficult to tell. But when a reporter from *Komsomolskaya Pravda* interviewed him in cordial fashion and the next day devoted a whole broadsheet page to being friendly about him, it began to be clear to us that in the long run Gorbachev would not be able to keep the genie of total control even in the vicinity of the bottle, let alone push him back inside. The next day, my husband was asked to lecture at Moscow University on the subject of V. I. Lenin, who had died soon enough after the Revolution to have escaped the unabated hatred of the Russian people for their Soviet revolutionary rulers and who was consequently held to be among the Russian heroes. Thus one day before we were to leave, the students of Moscow University were treated to an unsparing condemnation of both the ideas and the conduct of the man whose tomb in Red Square they had so piously continued to visit. Some members of the audience were red-faced angry, but some cheered. Could spring be far behind? We did not think so, truth to tell, but how glorious to have been proven needlessly pessimistic.

Moscow itself was predictably dingy and neglected, and long lines of people still stood patiently for hours to buy things: on one street corner people were waiting to buy tomatoes from a cardboard box, one to a customer, and outside a shop next to our hotel there was a line for three days, about which we learned that on the day of our arrival that shop had received a new shipment of men's undershirts. All this corresponded to what we had been hearing for years and thus took for granted.

But something else that no one had ever told me seemed to me to be a far more interesting symbol of people's lives under the Soviet government, and that was that wherever one went, there was only one unlocked door both to enter and exit by. And next to that door was a table, and at that table was sitting a bored and disgruntled servant of the Soviet government. This was true of hotels, of public buildings, of churches, of the Bolshoi Theater, and even of a shiny new mall building on the banks of the Moscow River named for the American industrialist Armand Hammer, in which, as in any proper mall, there were shops and offices. One door to go both in and out seems a handy way to keep track of people, and though clearly the surly person at the table no longer stopped, or even looked at, the people entering and leaving, it was a creepy reminder of what the words "government control" can really mean.

One of the Russian organizers of the conference had a delicious fifteen-year-old daughter, a little shy and freshly and unself-consciously pretty. She hung around with us a good deal and her English was very good, so I spent a fair amount of time talking to her. She was in high school, she told me, and mentioned one of her teachers who had been at our sessions, with her voice and face betraying what is recognizable everywhere in the world as a schoolgirl crush. When I asked her what was her favorite subject, she said philosophy. One of the particular horrors of the old Soviet Union was the combination of the clear superiority of its education (do American high-school girls even know how to spell "philosophy"?) and the decades-long inability of vast numbers of Soviet citizens to break out of their interior imprisonment. Except in the case of the true heroes among them, men like Vladimir Bukovsky, Natan Sharansky, and, of course, Alexander Solzhenitsyn, it would take the very dictator who dominated their lives to decree through the policy called glasnost that Russians were now to have minds of their own.

When I said good-bye to my young friend's father, I remarked to him, "You have a very beautiful and wonderful daughter." And knowing no better than we just how very soon the Soviet government would be falling apart, he answered, "Yes, but who knows what her future can possibly be?"

Who indeed? I thought of that girl a couple of weeks after our return, when I met a Russian émigré who was selling jewelry at a bazaar. She told me that in Moscow she had been a dentist but had discovered on arriving in the United States that all that she knew of dentistry the Americans had forgotten half a century before. I thought of my beautiful little friend, lover of philosophy, and suddenly grew angry all over again at the thought of all those self-regarding, undereducated American girls prating about their oppression.

As we were flying back to the United States after our seminar, something unforgettable happened. We had by the end been counting the minutes until we could get out of that place,

and thought "Oh, no" when we discovered that on the flight
with us was a group of American teenagers who had just spent
a month studying and touring as part of some U.S.-U.S.S.R.
cultural exchange program, while a group of their Russian
counterparts had been doing the same in the United States.
This particular exchange program had no doubt been devised
by one of those groups of clean-living, high-thinking citizens
who believe that helping peoples to know one another is the
great path to clearing up all misunderstandings and hence all
hostilities between them. If the program sponsors had been
with us on that flight, however, they might have been forced—
as we had been, for an opposite reason—to bethink themselves,
even if only a little. For just as soon as the plane began to lift
into the air, those American kids let out a great ear-splitting
cheer, whereupon one of their number shouted, "Don't cheer
just yet—we're still in their air space." So much for the influence on young minds of that great liberal nostrum, learning to
know another culture.

Now only a few short years later the great Eastern European
and Baltic breakup had reached its logical culmination in the
dissolution of the Soviet state, and there was someone in the
Kremlin about whose political tendencies we knew nothing
except that he had defeated his Communist predecessor. This,
of course, gave us leave to pin high hopes on Boris Yeltsin—
hopes that subsequently have, and at the same time have not at
all, been realized. And in the White House was Reagan's former vice president and successor, George Bush. About President Bush one thing was clear and one thing was unclear. What
was clear was that he was a kinder and more feeling man than

Ronald Reagan, and what was unclear was what he actually had in mind to do with his newfound power. (It soon became obvious that the answer to that was: very little.)

But if Bush, whose main interest was foreign policy, was now unclear, I was doubly so. The Committee for the Free World had been so much focused on Soviet Communism—both its power in the world and the culture in the United States to which a great fear of that power had given rise—that I wasn't sure what we should or could be doing now. One day I sat down to write the fund-raising letter that was sent each year to all our members and supporters, and as my pencil roamed over the foolscap (I was not yet computer literate), I could see that not one word on that page had the ring of truth to it. I realized that I would have to change the mission of the Committee just in order to keep it going. But who needed that? Neither the world nor I. So the very next morning I declared to my crestfallen staff that we would now be doing whatever it was that a tax-exempt educational organization had to do to shut down. And about six weeks later we stood on the street corner tearfully hugging one another good-bye and wondering what work each of us would find to do now.

I would soon discover that my closing down the Committee was considered by many to have been not only an unprecedented but a somehow brave and admirable thing to have done. Evidently, once it is in existence, no organization ever puts itself out of business. It certainly did not feel either brave or admirable to me. Rather, it just seemed pointless to change our entire agenda merely for the purpose of keeping on going. If anyone wanted to praise me for it, I would certainly not complain: praise is a commodity not easy to resist. But truth to tell, it was just that I had found the prospect of grinding on—for without the Soviet Union, that's how our work would have felt to us—too depressing.

The question of what I would do next, as the story of my life seems to me to make clear, was one about which I had always managed to maintain a certain degree of carelessness. For one thing, while practically no reasonably affluent woman in America, on pain of excommunication, would nowadays dare admit it, being a married woman removes a good deal of the urgency from the issue of finding work. Indeed, it may be that very lack of necessity that makes it difficult for so many educated married women to be content with the jobs they have. In my own case at least, ever since my children finished school and relieved us of tuition payments, I have been invited to do as I pleased with respect to finding paid employment. Nor can I possibly be alone in this. I used to tell people that I was a person of independent means, and when their eyebrows were raised sufficiently high, I would add by way of explanation, "I am a married woman."

But to do as one pleases, as anyone who has ever been in that position can tell you, is the hardest labor of all.

As it happened, I had only recently been administered a rare spiritual lesson—and from the unlikeliest of sources, my father. My father was a man who had spent his life willfully refusing to understand the simplest and most basic movements of the human heart, whether in himself or in others. After my mother died and he was left to live without the protection of the screen she had managed to interpose between him and the world, it became his constant occupation to badger the people close to him, especially his second wife, two of his three daughters, and even, when the opportunity presented itself, his grandchildren. My relations with both my parents had been tense enough

when my mother was alive: they could never figure out what I
was up to and never knew whether to be pleased or outraged
by what had become of me. And after my mother's death, I
managed politely and with all due propriety to stay as far out of
my father's target range as possible. I had not for years, maybe
never, been a properly dutiful daughter, but I think it not unfair
to say that at certain critical moments he on his side had also
been a far from properly dutiful father. Be that as it may, he was
an incredibly vigorous man, to my stepmother's bitter disap-
pointment refusing to retire from his business until he was close
to ninety, and he was even then up for traveling to many a far-
off place. If his body gave him trouble, no one would ever have
been informed of it. He and my stepmother bought an apartment in Miami to winter in, and damned if he, virtually deaf
and with eyesight dangerously far from acute, didn't take the
Florida driving test time after time until he won the prize of a
driver's license. At God knows what peril to those on the road
with him.

Then one summer day I was informed that he was in the
hospital in Minnesota, dying. He was ninety-two. He had
come back from a trip to Israel with a cough he couldn't shake,
and this cough turned out to be the symptom of a well-
advanced cancer of the liver. As soon as I heard, I called him on
the phone in his hospital room. "What on earth did you go and
do to yourself?" I asked him in the bantering tone we had finally learned to use with one another to keep any possible
storm from brewing. His answer to me was the greatest gift he
ever had, or ever could have, given me. "Who am I," he
answered, "to be spared the pleasures that are given to
everyone?"

By the time I found a flight and got myself to the hospital,
he had already drifted off into unconsciousness and had noth-

ing more to say to the world. But to me he had already said everything I could ever have needed him to say.

Less than a year later—everybody said it was a mercy that my father was now comfortably in his grave—my oldest sister and her husband were killed in a hotel fire in Cairo, Egypt. It seems that it had taken the Egyptian fire trucks more than half an hour to show up in the middle of the night, by which time the whole hotel was up in flames, and it seems further that the hotel management may in the meantime have been less than scrupulous about waking all the guests and getting them out of the place. Anyway, the pair were found in the hallway just outside their door, side by side, clutching their passports. They were meticulous that way, never leave your hotel without your passport, which was weirdly lucky for us because they would otherwise have been unrecognizable. Even so, we had to send the American embassy in Cairo copies of their dental records before the identification could be made official.

They were childless, and they had named me their personal representative, which meant that I was to be responsible for overseeing the execution of their will. Once again I would spend clumps of time in Washington, where they had been living, this time disposing of their apartment and all their many, many things—the two of them having turned out to be assiduous collectors of books, papers, objects, paintings, and even clothes. It was an unholy job: I felt every moment as if I were violating their privacy and somehow trampling on what had been their so carefully tended life. And all around me people were saying equally unholy things, the gist of which was that it was lucky at least that they had died together. Two deaths better than one—how consoling. I knew that they didn't really mean anything by saying what they did, those who spoke this way; but the spiritual illiteracy of so many perfectly nice people left me almost as depressed as the painful job it had fallen to me to do.

But if it was spiritual literacy I was looking for, I would soon be put in the way of a veritable banquet of it. For when all the affairs of the Committee for the Free World were finally settled (it is easy to start something, but legally as well as emotionally very trying to bring it to an end), I found myself moving to a new home. Once many years earlier I had had a long and deliciously alcohol-filled lunch with an old friend named Richard Neuhaus. Richard was then a Lutheran pastor, but at that point pastoral work had become a kind of sideline while he was directing an institute devoted to introducing—or rather reintroducing—religion into American public life. In his view—and mine, and the view of a whole group of our political companions—the meaning of the First Amendment had been entirely corrupted by liberal secular interpreters so that what was intended to ensure that the United States government could not establish a single official religion had come to be used as a means for banishing religion itself. He had written a very important book titled *The Naked Public Square,* and this image of an entirely emptied and secularized American public life had taken hold powerfully among many of us who were worried about the moral condition of our public institutions.

At the end of this lunch, he said to me, "Maybe you will come and hang out with us some day," which was pleasant, and neither of us gave it a second thought. Many adventures were passed by both of us after that conversation. We had our respective successes and our battles. Then one day I learned that he had converted from Lutheranism to Catholicism, a move that surely delighted the Church; that I as a Jew found no more than rather curious and quite interesting; and that a good number (though not all) of his former Lutheran confreres took an extremely dim view of. And around that same time, as I was wondering what besides disposing of my sister's worldly goods I would do now, he invited me to come and hang around as a fellow of his Institute on Religion and Public Life. His lunchtime invitation had come round again, and this time I accepted with pleasure. Neither he nor I had any firm idea of what I would be doing as a "fellow," but since the Institute published a magazine, called *First Things,* I supposed that at least I could offer some service there. The editor of the magazine, Jim Nuechterlein, was also an old friend, so I was quite sure he would not view me as any kind of hostile interloper.

Thus one morning I arrived at the office of the Institute on Religion and Public Life, startled to find Richard sitting in an ordinary shirt and wearing an ordinary-to-a-fault necktie. (He would be ordained a priest about a year after his conversion, and could then return to wearing a proper collar.) The staff was just the way I had grown to like it, which is to say, tiny: Richard's executive assistant, a receptionist, and aside from Jim Nuechterlein, who has remained a determined Lutheran, a young Jew named Matt Berke, who was the magazine's managing editor. I was given a grand office, far grander than the one I had given myself at the Committee, and made welcome in every possible way.

But then began an ordeal, fully compensated for by the new friendships and associations my position would bring into my life, but an ordeal nevertheless. It had to do with vocabulary— a rather important fixture in the life of a writer and editor— and mine had all of a sudden become feeble. I was now living in a community of religious thinkers whose language was often about as familiar to me as the dialect of an African tribe. I found myself running into Jim's office virtually every day, saying, "Jim, quick. Tell me what *kerygma* means." Or, "*propaedeutic.*" Or, "————." Jim was amused by my discomfiture, and I suppose Richard was as well, though I think he could never credit just how ignorant I was. Anyway, here I found myself, well into my sixties, rushing like a schoolgirl to the dictionary and like a schoolgirl again, almost immediately forgetting the definition I had found there.

But if life at the Institute could sometimes be a kind of Christian ordeal for this only half-educated Jew, there were things I had known and done and seen that could sometimes be of value to the enterprise. And I could at the very least amuse and scandalize my colleagues with long-ago gossip from the literary community I had departed twenty-five years earlier.

Another odd and sometimes rather disquieting thing was going on with me because of my presence at the Institute and the deepening friendships I was finding there. That is, that I was being forced to think through and articulate positions on issues that had for years basically been allowed to swim around somewhere beneath the top of my consciousness. One of these issues was that complex of problems that had come, oversimply, to be called "family values." It is true that over the years I had earned some attention, a good deal of it enraged, as an unyielding opponent of the women's movement, and much of my opposition had had to do with that movement's assault on marriage. But on the other hand, I myself had been divorced, and with two small children to boot. How could I in good conscience stand up in public and oppose divorce, especially since I had not only broken up my marriage but never doubted that I had saved my life by doing so? It was my second marriage that taught me the real meaning of family—too late to have done a whole lot for my generally undutiful behavior as a child but perhaps at just the right time to have taught me a few important things about being a parent. How was I to say all this and yet be of use as a forthright opponent of the country's "easy come, easy go, whatever suits you" culture?

I am also in principle opposed to abortion, and yet I can easily visualize circumstances when I could not find it within myself to offer my objection to a woman determining to have one. Should a mother of young children, for instance, be threatened with death if she were to carry a pregnancy to full term (this, I believe, is the Jewish view: if the choice is between mother or child, choose the mother); or if, as happened to an acquaintance, a woman were to hold a dying Tay-Sachs infant in her arms day and night for months while he, blind and unable to hear, could do nothing but scream in pain, and she were then to discover from amniocentesis that she was pregnant with another Tay-Sachs baby. The answer to me, I know, is that hard cases make bad law, but when it comes to certain kinds of human dilemmas, I can't help but feel that hard law can sometimes also make bad cases. Abortion should of course be illegal, but not, as was the case before Roe *v.* Wade, absolutely impossible under all conditions. Again, my view is one far too complicated to be useful on the hustings against cries such as the old famous "It's my body; I can do what I want with it."

One important contribution I could without any complication make to the work of my friends at the Institute on Religion and Public Life, and that was as a Jew. It was no secret that some significant part in the emptying of the public square had been played by Jewish liberals. It was understandable to me why this was so, because their long history had left many Jews with a deep atavistic fear of Christian authority—so the more public life could be kept strictly secular the safer they felt. But understand it or not, I believed that the religion-free public condition to which they had made such a vital contribution had left American society, and particularly American culture, vulnerable to pernicious influences. About the security and survival of the State of Israel I would brook not even a hint of hemming or hawing in my presence, but when it came to the liberal Jewish hostility to conservative Christianity I had not the slightest hesitation about going public with my whole-hearted opposition. They might have been warming them-selves with their sense of their own public virtue, those liberals, but in my view if they continued to have their way, they would be leaving their offspring, and ours, in a society overrun with cultural barbarians masquerading as the Enlightenment. My de-fending the conservative Christians to the Jews was naturally bound to have a greater impact—if only by virtue of the shock of it—than their own.

About a year from the time of his conversion to Catholi-cism, Richard was ordained a priest, and many of his friends, including my husband and me, attended the ordination, which took place in the chapel of a seminary in a nearby suburb. Later there was much joshing among his old buddies who professed their pleasure and amazement at seeing Richard lying prone before his Maker, and other such niceties. But as for me, I was fascinated by the mass (not my first but by a mile the most solemn), especially for some reason by the incense, and it oc-curred to me that while Richard was already becoming an in-fluential Catholic thinker, it might take longer than a year for a lifelong Lutheran to become a fingertips-and-nervous-system Catholic.[1]

Richard was soon to become very ill, partly because life had decreed that he, too, was not to be spared certain of its "plea-

---

1. I write this something like a decade later. It did, and he has.

sures," and partly out of sheer medical neglect. That is, his condition was allowed by his doctor (happily his doctor no longer) to become near fatal before proper attention was paid to it, whereupon rather drastic surgery was required. He later told us that on the operating table he had the near-death experience of hearing heavenly voices tell him that his death was being postponed but that all was being held in readiness for him.

So my spiritual instruction went on apace, first through my father's peaceful surrender to death and then through Richard's loving surrender to life.

My time at the Institute on Religion and Public Life, as at a couple of other happy places, was to be five years. (It seems I always managed to clear out at the point where there would be pleasant memories on both sides.) This time I was retiring for good, because my husband had made up his mind that thirty-five years of being the editor of *Commentary* was enough: he would reach his sixty-fifth birthday in January of 1995, and by May of that year he would be packed up and gone. He had succeeded in naming his successor, Neal Kozodoy, someone in whose hands he was happy and grateful to be leaving the magazine, had a farewell celebration attended by hundreds of his friends, and headed for a theoretical "sunset." And I of course headed with him. "Whither thou goest go I," said the lady.

For most people, the word "retirement" conjures up images of wintering in the sun, summering on a golf course, and in between, touring the world. For my husband, however, retirement has primarily meant dividing his days between his computer and his stereo equipment (and lovely things have been coming out of both). In New York City, his "office" has been half of a rather large bedroom, in which there has been little hope of getting him set up properly, but since we have both taken a solemn oath that the only way either of us will be moved from our apartment is in a pine box, there is little we can do to improve the situation.

For years, however, we had had a shack at the beach, which had again, summer or winter, been more a place of work than of play for him. But it was time, facing our sunset years, to have a grown-up house in which to spend the time away from our city home—and in which he could for once have decent working conditions. So we did something no one would have believed of us: we sold our shack and built ourselves a very large and pleasant house—large enough, indeed, to accommodate a goodly number of children and grandchildren. And to the astonishment of two confirmed urban apartment dwellers, we discovered how pleasant it can be to live, not to mention have guests, in very large spaces (when he is at his desk, and I at mine, we communicate with walkie-talkies).

We sometimes also in our comfortable sunset years contemplate a strange injustice in human affairs, to wit: when you are young and have growing children, your need for money and the amenities money can buy is far greater and far more intensely felt than when you are old; and yet for most people it is only when their children are grown that they begin to collect the real winnings of their lifetime of work. Life has arranged it so they have more and at the same time there is less call on their resources.

Their financial resources, that is. As one's children grow older, and one's grandchildren become people to reckon with instead of creatures to cuddle, one's spiritual resources if anything get drawn on more than ever. Each child, each grandchild, has his own life to live and his own story to tell, and yet each, willy-nilly, remains on one's emotional books day in and day out forever.

About this time I found myself as a conservative being invited by various groups to lecture about family "values"[2] but actually just trying to say only what I myself happen to have been taught by life about families. (An odd circumstance, since after all, I was not only divorced when I had two young children, I happen also to be the approving mother of the divorces of each of my children, and thus can hardly constitute a model for what they call the "traditional" family.) One thing I do know for sure about families, however, and it was this that I was mainly trying to say about them: children and grandchildren keep you both anchored in the everydayness of life and safely out of the fever swamps of Self. This may not sound like much, but it is something that can take a long time to come to understand.

Family, however, was far from the only thing I had come to be speaking out about. For something like thirty years I have found myself inveighing against the tendency of the country's so-called morally superior people to excuse black criminals for their crimes, regarding the wrongdoers' race alone as grounds for their exoneration. Such people do not seem to realize that what they are saying—and what many a black so-called "leader" is urging them to say—is that because some thug or rapist is black and participates on that account in a long history of suffering, he can't be expected to know better. This is what

2. In his *The Closing of the American Mind,* the late Allan Bloom explained to me why I have always so hated the word "values." For one thing, it gets people off the hook of having to speak about "truth," and for another, it has all my life been used by people I know to declare their superiority to others.

they say, and then move themselves as far away from where black people live, or hang out, as their pocketbooks can carry them. Such, for instance, was the running argument that occupied more than one visit to my hometown, with people who had no black friends and certainly no black neighbors and whose only image of the lives of black people was entirely operatic, requiring operatic attitudes in return. That is precisely why people like Jesse Jackson and his heir apparent, the Reverend Al Sharpton, have been able to exploit their black brothers for the purpose of wringing special favors out of nervous white people—corporations and politicians and movie stars preeminently, but just plain fine folk as well. No one likes to hear anyone say such things, of course: they can't figure out if I am a racist, in which case they could happily condemn me, but unfortunately it is I who am calling *them* racist. I keep wondering how many generations of little black kids will have to go on living terrorized and squelched by the violence all around them in order to burnish the "compassion" of such people.

Nor have I been able to understand—and I continue to say so in public—how that most virulent of all sexually transmitted diseases called AIDS can have become the occasion for so many intelligent people's falling in love with homosexuality. In song and story, not to say hugely successful plays and musicals, nothing seems to move certain people so much as the beatification of someone who is dying a ghastly death because of what they choose to call his "lifestyle"—as if engaging in various sorts of life-threatening sexual practices is like so much home furnishing.

Like the women's movement in the seventies, the homosexual rights movement in the nineties has carried all public (and much private) discourse before it. But again, as with the women's movement in the seventies, one can hope that the country's homosexuals will recover their senses, return to their own private lives, abjure the bathhouses and gay-bar back rooms and the faceless couplings that take place there, and resist the horror that has befallen so many of their friends and loved ones. For the cultural embrace of AIDS by the homosexuals' artistic champions and "straight" sentimentalizers betokens nothing so much as a frivolous but nevertheless dangerous embrace of death. The very opposite, you might say, of the principle of family—divorce and all.

After doing untold damage to courtship and marriage, and taking the heart out of this society's treatment of little boys, the women's movement seems little by little to be quietly stealing away. But of the war for what nowadays passes as "civil rights"—that is, setting black children back educationally by pointlessly assaulting an already somewhat shaky public school system, placing heavily black communities at the continuing mercy of thugs and criminals with their constant barrage against police power, and breeding a terrible skepticism about black achievement with demands for special treatment—those who claim its generalship now seem merely to be feeding contentedly on their own celebrity.

And as for the homosexual rights movement, it is too soon to say what future course it might take. For now, having come to wield an enormous influence over the country's sex-education curricula, the next move seems to be pursuit of the right to be legally married. At the moment, it seems that no one but the really hard-bitten seems to be able to say them nay. In short, the movement is in full flood. However, we hear that the spread of HIV is up again among homosexual men, which has to mean that they are once again up to their dangerous habits—as if in defiance of life itself. Why they should wish to endanger themselves this way when little by little society is giving way to their demands is a very real question. Perhaps—who knows?—in some deeply psychological sense they play with death *because* society is putting up so little resistance to their demands.

These things, too, I have now and then over the years made so bold as to write and lecture about. As the reader can imagine, then, among my adventures could be counted no awarding of medals. Still, as the years wear on, at least I find myself less and less alone in my opinions.

~10~

Girls Fleeing Freedom

WITH THE ACTIVIST PHASE of feminism definitely on the wane, now something else was happening. We were beginning to hear a new kind of message from a younger group of women, who had been brought up to be both granddaughters in good standing of the sexual revolution and at the same time unquestioning products of the women's movement. (To place these young women among the generations as quickly as I know how, I would say they are too young to be my children and too old to be my grandchildren—in other words, students in college in the late eighties and early nineties.) They had been conditioned to take entirely for granted without even arguing the case their right to be in and out of as many beds as they pleased, while at the same time they had also imbibed—with their mothers' milk, as it were—those views of the women's movement that held the sexual revolution to be part and parcel of women's oppression. And what they had begun to tell us about themselves at once both reassured and deeply saddened me. For they had begun to resist the idea that they felt just as easygoing about sexual promiscuity as the young men in their lives, and what reassured me was that despite the near-lethal combined influence of social science, the entertainment industry, and advertising, human nature remains human nature, recognizable beneath all the detritus of public discourse. What saddened me, on the other hand, was the problem of how very hurtful are the means these young women have been left with to find their way through to what they really feel.

Back in the late sixties, when the women's movement was new, I had paid very close attention to it. From reading and listening, it became clear to me then that the angry and often downright vicious attacks being leveled against men by the movement's ideologists had far more to do with an impulse to escape from sexual freedom than with the desire simply to share in men's worldly power. There was a sly, probably even unconscious, maneuver involved here, however. Because for the women's liberationists to have said, "We have now tried this sleeping around for a few years and we cannot stand it" would have meant becoming reactionaries in the literal sense of the term. And to find oneself in league with the backward-looking, if only in this one respect, was psychologically and spiritually out of the question. For they were after all liberal— and many of them to the left of that—to the core. The only way remaining to them was to declare a revolution—a revolution against that vast collectivity called men the oppressors.

Now here were their daughters in college, with none of their mothers' once-upon-a-time uncertainty about their "roles" in the world but nevertheless left, still angry, in the same old quandary about men. The young men in their corner of the world had, of course, long since been brought to heel in all sorts of ways—most especially in their habits of speech—but since they had evidently not been sexually disabled—thank God for the unmanageable energies of youth!—the girls were left with the same old problem, now much intensified: how to get off the sexual merry-go-round and at the same time keep their bona fides as fully enlightened young women.

Oh, the mind has mountains, said Gerard Manley Hopkins. With the aid of a handful of thoroughly inflamed elders, the new generation hit upon a system that would assist them in feeling chaste without having to take responsibility for being so. Which is to say, they came upon the idea of "date rape." According to this most ingenious invention, if, for instance, a young woman drinks too much, goes off to bed with some young man, and rues having done so in the morning, she may allow herself to claim that she had been raped. The ground for this is that having been drunk, she had not truly given her consent; she had been taken advantage of against her will. Or perhaps she had not been drunk, had said yes, but had changed her mind when it was too late—that, too, might be considered rape. It is not that there has ceased to be such a thing as actual rape, a crime of violence against women helpless before superior force, but the definition had become so expanded as to render young women entirely nonresponsible for their own behavior, no matter how stupid or careless. For instance, that she was in some room in a frat house, dead drunk or zonked on drugs, may not be taken to mean that she was, as they say, "asking for it," but on the other hand, it also does not mean that she was no more than an innocent victim, either.

In 1975, one Susan Brownmiller, a leading feminist, published a book called *Against Our Will* whose thesis, when boiled down to the basics, was that sexual intercourse itself is rape *by its very nature.* Pleased as the Libbers were to regard her as one of their own, I imagine that only the most extreme of the extremists bought her actual analysis. But now Miss Brownmiller's younger sisters had brilliantly revived the idea of rape in a way that enabled them to carry a whole army of contemporaries with them: to wit, rape was something which happened when any young woman determined that it had. A most dazzling example of this was the story reported some years ago by the *New York Times* about a young woman who called the cops and claimed to have been raped after she had invited a younger boy to take off his clothes, enter the bed where she lay naked, and spend the night with her there. She had not, after all, she said, given him permission to have sex with her.

In the early nineties the idea of date rape caught fire on just about every college campus across the land. Possibly things went the farthest at Antioch College, where there was issued a set of rules governing the sexual behavior of the school's male students according to which for each additional advance made to a female, permission must be asked and granted. First for a kiss, then for a fondle, then for the opening of a button, then the opening of a hook-and-eye, and so on, all the way to consummation. It's hard to imagine the young man—or young girl, for that matter—who would not at some point most urgently find the need to break through the system in order to ask and grant several permissions at once, and there was much joking about the whole thing on the part of a good many people who heard about it. But not, evidently, at Antioch, where, we were told, the new rules were taken by many if not most with the utmost seriousness.

In other places the young women have engaged in actual celebrations of their having been date-raped. In her book *The Morning After,* published in 1993, the gifted young writer Katie

Roiphe describes such celebrations at both Harvard and Princeton, where she had respectively been an undergraduate and a graduate student. In both these schools—and, it would appear, in many others—the ritual is called "Take Back the Night" and involves a veritable army of female students, accompanied by a few sympathetic males, who parade around the campus miming rage and shouting. In Princeton, the parading stops at several predesignated places while various volunteers stand up before a microphone and tell the assemblage the stories of their own "rape experiences." Sometimes they weep—and sometimes, according to Katie Roiphe, in order to be in on the party they tell plain lies—and a great catharsis is had by all.

Miss Roiphe herself deeply disapproves of the invention of date rape on the ground that it represents a serious form of abdication of responsibility for one's own decisions and conduct. But in her analysis of this new invention, persuasive as it is, even she continues to leave one shoe undropped: she does not seem to take much time considering the possibility that young women might simply choose to give up the game of sex entirely until it were once again to cease being no more than a passing entertainment and paid the respect due to something consequential. (At least at the time she wrote this book, such a possibility seems to have remained quite beyond her ken.)

Fortune has evidently provided these young women with another barrier to sex besides the idea of rape, namely, HIV and AIDS. Despite there being no evidence that plain vanilla sexual intercourse between two heterosexuals can result in AIDS, fear of contracting the disease seems to be a common topic of conversation among the young. To be sure, their high-school sex-education courses had already been trying to impress upon them that they were in grave danger; and in New York City, to take one example, for several years now the advertising placards in the subway cars have been carrying a running comic strip in both Spanish and English that follows the unhappy fortune of an ordinary young Hispanic woman who discovers that she has sexually transmitted HIV and must tell her young man about it. This particular falsehood serves a double purpose. First, it provides young women with a possible source of resistance to having sex that their upbringing has insistently failed to provide; and second, it helps to promote the idea—so evidently untrue and at the same time so sisterly and charitable to their homosexual friends—that everyone is equally at risk of contracting AIDS. In any case, if one can believe Miss Roiphe, many girls keep their own supply of condoms and sometimes insist that their partners use two of them at a time (a romantic interlude if ever there was one).

Interestingly, it is other kinds of sexually transmitted diseases that by all accounts are spreading and that the use of two condoms might reasonably be meant to keep at bay. The fear of pregnancy—once the great preventive for young women in danger of succumbing to the heat of the moment—is not given a single mention. (Nor is the fact that there are other and probably more effective means of contraception, which, however, unhappily for our coeds, do require a woman's assuming full responsibility.) According to the medical statistics one reads about, while AIDS does not really apply, except to intravenous drug users, genital herpes, lifelong and incurable though far from fatal, certainly does. As for pregnancy, no doubt cheap and easy abortion has made it seem of small consequence. In any case, the point is that between the alleged claim of rape and the alleged fear of AIDS, an unacknowledged counterpressure to unhindered sexual freedom is a-building. Call it the new New Chastity.

Katie Roiphe charges that the idea of date rape involves the abdication of personal responsibility on the part of all the young women who have latched onto it, and there is no doubt that she is right. But that is only the beginning of an understanding of the problem. For these young women are harboring an inner disturbance they have been left with no means of confronting, let alone giving honest expression to. The unacknowledged truth is that most of them do not wish to sleep around, and they do not wish to be granted permission to do so. Which is to say, they need backing of some kind, from parents, schools, cultural authorities, but wherever they turn these days, such backing is denied them. They cry "rape" when they know full well that they have not been raped because deep down they feel that the world around them has denied them the means to resist in any other way.

Most people, especially young people, need to be confirmed by the community in which they live. They cannot beyond a certain limit establish for themselves a system of their own verities and preferences. This is as true of the members of the most posh country club as it is of the boys hanging around on a ghetto street corner. And it has been decreed for some time now that except for meting out punishment for speech that is deemed offensive by one group or another, the colleges take no responsibility for the social conduct of their students. This could in fact be put more strongly: arranging it so that male and female students share common dormitory floors and bathrooms, as schools commonly do these days, is not so much a lack of restriction as a positive invitation. That for those living in such nonrestrictive dorms sharing common bathrobe, shower, and toothbrush moments may very well be more of a sexual turnoff than a provocation is nothing to the point, which is, that the school will have no part in what happens. Either way, in other words, to them it is no big deal.

In *The Closing of the American Mind* Allan Bloom made a great point about the use of the above expression, "no big deal," among his students. It distressed him greatly, he said, when in their discussions with him they spoke those words most particularly in response to his bringing up the subject of love and romance. He was right to be distressed, of course. "No big deal" are words that positively chill the blood when they are meant that way. But let it be said of the young that they are being surrounded, and well instructed, by an army of experts at chilling people's blood.

So one has to feel anxiety for those girls who must claim to have been raped in order to have some ground on which to resist feeling coerced by their community into doing what they actually do not wish to do. In other words, it's hard to call off the sexual revolution. Aside from the conservative Christian community, which has never really been involved in this problem except through the expression of its stern opposition, only a few stalwart souls have thus far publicly declared their intention to do so. Miss Wendy Shalit, for instance, in a recent book called *A Return to Modesty* is engaged in a counterrevolution by means of reviving the idea of female maidenliness. But aside from a call to resistance here and there, for the present the idea of masculine-style sexual freedom for women is now too deeply ingrained in the culture of the educated middle class to be confronted head on by anyone but those with an appetite for verbal armed struggle. So for now young women are making do with marching around angrily, shaking their fists, and telling one another untrue stories about how they were raped.

All this would be fascinating to watch, for old Mother Nature has a very large bag of tricks through which to make

herself known. One day for certain the world of the enlightened will witness some new disposition of the relations between the sexes. But meanwhile it makes me nervous, because
I have granddaughters who not all that long from now will be
thrown into the sexual whirl and whichever way they turn, are
liable to be made unhappy by it. One granddaughter, indeed,
has recently gone off to college. As it happens, she is someone
who is not likely to do anything she feels is against the better
angels of her own nature—at least she has not been seen to do
so since she took what were virtually her first steps. (I can't
help thinking that the war of wills she often exhausted her
mother with in those years is paying my daughter off handsomely now.) But she happens to be going off to one of those
cozy small places that can be very lonely without at least a small
society of kindred spirits.

There is a sense, to be sure, in which none of what I worry
about in connection with my granddaughters is any of my business. These girls have mothers and fathers who keep very close
and loving eyes on them; and it is their parents' job to do the
worrying, as I once put in my time doing over them. (Number
three granddaughter lives in Jerusalem, where such problems as
the one I described are liable to seem like a luxury in view of
all the other things about which one has to fear for one's child
in that city.) By my reckoning a grandmother is supposed to be
merely the furniture in which a child finds perpetual comfort,
like an old overstuffed sofa. But still, I can't help having my
own hopes—call them prayers—for these girls (for my grandsons I have hopes, or prayers, as well, but they are entirely different ones). I would hate for them to have to become prigs in
order to be able to stay out of the current system of displeas-
ing social-sexual pressure. I would hate for them to have to
lose out on all the fun, and Sturm und Drang, of flirtation

and rehearsal for romance, for these are the ways that young women actually discover their true and proper power over men. How sad it is that the movement claiming to liberate women and give them control over their own lives should have adopted a program in which they deprive females of one of the most significant means of tasting power and control. All the law and medical degrees in the world will not make up for what women have been losing in their relations with men, for to become tough and demanding as feminism has defined the process of their taking control is as nothing compared with being hungered for and, later on in life, indispensable.

I have no way of saying such things to these girls for whom I would cheerfully give my life. I could not in fact say them convincingly, or perhaps even comprehensibly, to their mothers when they were girls, for I myself was young then and too much in the thick of battle—caught between the party of the self-righteous and that of the sinners and trying to carry the fight to both. And now, somehow, I am too old not to be affectionately patronized as "out of it."

The women of Princeton and just about every other college and university in the land were not only spending their time "taking back the night," they were also participating in a massive general corruption of American higher education. Back in the early 1980s, when I was reading college catalogues as part of the cultural warfare being conducted by the Committee for the Free World, a year's tuition in a top-rated private college was on average twenty thousand dollars per year—which, when one factors in all extraneous expenses, particularly transportation, actually added up to close to thirty thousand dollars all told. By the year 2000 it was considerably higher, having increased in some places by nearly 50 percent! This means that families, even well-off ones, with two children in college at the same time—as will soon be the case with two of my own daughters—will be sending some institution or institutions a very significant chunk of their earnings. Others will go deeply into debt, mortgaging their houses, for instance, to pay for what everyone nowadays knows is essential to insure a kid an even minimally decent future.

And except for the scientifically or technologically talented, who focus on a specialization from the beginning, what are these students being taught? The answer, with the exception of only a few honorable holdout schools, is damn all, unless the students themselves make a concerted and countercultural effort to learn. Black students, for instance, are allowed to get a degree in the study of their oppression, as women students are in theirs. Students of English are given reading lists to make the hair stand on end—mostly a lot of second-, if not third-, rate recent novels displaying "correct" social attitudes with maybe one or two serious modern works thrown in, nothing too demanding. Those who advance beyond this fare and reach the point of serious literary studies are taught such enlightening modes of analysis as that nothing means or signifies beyond what readers determine for themselves that it does. Students of modern history are given a thorough understanding of the crimes committed by, for, and within the United States of America, as are, of course, by means of a somewhat different vocabulary, students of sociology.

America's young women were once upon a time in American history known to be their country's indispensable civilizing force. Under God knows what conditions of hardship they made their way to a vast western wilderness and made it habitable, both for themselves and for those who were to come after, by insistently turning it into a place of schools and families

and churches. Now thanks to much progress in the affairs of
women, their feminine descendants may have reached that
striven-for and blessed condition of equality where they can be
just as blindly driven and spiritually uncouth as any fron-
tiersman.

As for my grandsons, I think it unlikely that any of them will
ever be found signing on to some men's group engaged in supporting the "rights"—read demands—of women. Nor, on the
other hand, are they one day likely to be sitting around camp-
fires beating drums and trying to recapture their hunter-gath-
erer roots. (The Israelis are perhaps an exception, as their mere
citizenship requires their participation in some of the most serious rituals of manhood there are.)

It looks to me as if the five eldest of them are already showing unmistakable signs of hungering for girls, though naturally
not all with the same degree of assurance about their eventual
success in the quest. What do I want for them? That their relations with girls add to their feeling of being strengthened and
enriched, and not in the end prove to be a drag upon their
spirits. I am aware that in the minds of some there would seem
to be a contradiction between what I hope for my grandsons
and what I hope for their sisters. But there isn't really. For the
health and vitality of relations between men and women depend precisely on there being a truly friendly adjudication of
what respectively meets the honestly recognized needs of both.

It takes a while, and a certain amount of growing up on both
sides, for this to happen. And in the meantime, I watch and
hope.

~11~

To Startle This
Dull Pain

HOPING GOES ON FOREVER. But sticking around in this world in order to keep on doing it seems to be another matter. Or so anyway we are told and warned and scolded by the Health Police from morning to night.

Thus among the various things that have lately been imposed on people of retirement age is the adoption of at least one regular regimen of physical exercise—two would naturally be even better. (There is usually also a certain daily ration of pills of various kinds, but of those the less said the better.) Living in New York City as I do, I walk a great deal, but according to the H.P. walking doesn't count unless it is very strenuous and one doesn't stop for traffic. Having tried, and from the sheer boredom of it rejected, a stationary bicycle, a few years ago I gratefully latched onto the idea of swimming, for that was something I had long ago done fairly well and with a good deal of pleasure. Even this I would never have undertaken, however—being generally sunk in the sin of sloth as I am—had it not been for a friend who was also seeking some nonmechanical form of exercise and had also thought of swimming. She quickly agreed to serve as my exercise conscience if I would agree to serve as hers. And so to this day, unless something more pressing intervenes, swim we do, half a mile twice a week in an excellent Olympic-sized community pool nearby, moaning and groaning and counting the laps all the way. And it turns out that while swimming for pleasure in the lakes of Minnesota, or in the icy brine of the Atlantic Ocean on the eastern end of Long Island, can offer much pleasure, swimming laps for exercise is little more than another form of tedium, admittedly less grueling than the bicycle machine (my friend, who will certainly live forever, does both).

Among the other regulars at the pool are groups of young girls from various nearby private schools who are members of their respective schools' swimming teams doing an early-morning workout. Often they are dressing to get to school just as we are undressing to put on our swimming suits. They seem to be anywhere from thirteen to sixteen years old—though naturally these days in the case of adolescent girls it is difficult to discern any difference between one age and another. On the days that we and they find ourselves in the locker room together, my friend and I cannot help but overhear their conversation. For they do, the young, tend to speak to one another in full voice, even if they generally speak to their elders in a low murmur.

My friend is irritated to a fare-thee-well by their grammar and syntax, or rather lack of same, and makes fun of the way they begin every sentence with the word "like." After all, she says, it is costing their parents a pretty penny for them to be conditioned to speak as if they were illiterate. I, on the other hand, am more fascinated by what they are talking *about,* for they appear to have only one topic of conversation: not, as you might expect, boys, not clothes, not their putatively unmanageable hair or their out-of-proportion bodies or anything that girls their age used to be preoccupied with. On the contrary, they talk almost exclusively about . . . their mothers: "Do you know what she said to me last night?" "Did I tell you what she plans to do?" "Can you imagine what her latest bright idea is?" "You should have seen what she was wearing when she went out last night!" And so on.

I listen and try to picture for myself these mothers who are so central to their daughters' preoccupations. They are probably in their mid-to-late forties or perhaps early fifties, well heeled (for tuition in these schools has grown way beyond what people like us were once able to scrape together), stylish as prosperous women nowadays almost certainly are, and given to the kind of enlightened attitudes that are generally predictable among women of their age and circumstance. What is it that gives them a position of such prominence among their daughters' girlish preoccupations? It cannot be that they are mean to their children or frighteningly stern—their culture would not permit that. It cannot on the other hand be that they are so utterly indifferent to their children as to fill them with longing for some unattainable love—they were much too intent on adding motherhood to the accoutrements of their lives for that.

But why should I be so concerned? After all, I've made my pile: three young granddaughters, each of whom stands on her own two feet in her own inimitable way. Perhaps it is just that keeping my eye on women, and girls who become women, is an old habit of mine. Perhaps on the other hand it is no more than a form of worrying about my American grandsons, for these are the girls, at least by age and social circumstance, whom life is preparing for them.

Whatever the occasion for my curiosity about them, one thing seems clear to me: these girls are in some way terribly needy children. By their age, one's mother ought to be someone who, for good or ill, can be taken quite for granted. A pain in the ass, perhaps, a nuisance surely, or possibly even a mere figure of fun, but a fixture in one's life requiring no special attention—let alone the kind of attention that in one's early teens is supposed to be reserved for boys, clothes, the unfairness of teachers, and skin blemishes.

Now, these girls have little in common with that particular cohort of female teenagers who are both aggressive and filthy-mouthed and can be counted on to jostle one in the New York City subways around three o'clock every afternoon, though they do tend to be rather careless about the rights of others with whom they share the dressing room and they do tend to leave a terrible mess behind them. Nor do they use obscenity to punctuate everything they say, as one hears has become commonplace among many of their age and social standing, though perhaps it is our presence that inhibits them. In any case, the point is that they seem to be perfectly ordinary, semi-literate, not unattractive, upper-middle-class kids. Except, that is, for this unaccountable, highly suspect preoccupation with their mothers.

Something seems to have gone amiss with that thread of mother-love that lets children venture inquisitively out into the world knowing they always have a way back to safety. The young girls on whose conversation I have been eavesdropping, whatever their affectations of maturity, must not feel safe. Now, it cannot be that that maternal thread has simply been broken: only a maddened ideologue deaf to the workings of the human heart could come to the conclusion that my locker-room mates, as a group, are simply unwanted and unloved. What I believe has happened in their case is that the thread of security has been let out to such an unmanageable length that they feel the necessity of staying focused on their starting point, lest they never be able to find their way back home.

At my pool, either they are, as I said, inhibited by the presence of two grandmotherly ladies, or perhaps, needy though they clearly are, they are not quite as bereft as a goodly number of their schoolmates. For there have been some truly hair-raising reports about other groups of private-high-school girls very like them who are suffering—they themselves, of course, might call it enjoying—such a distance from safety that one cannot imagine what the future holds for them.

Two things in particular suggest the measure of that distance. First are the downtown nightclubs in which, since theoretically no alcohol is served to them, they are allowed to hang out, maybe pick up boys, and dance the night away. One of the ways in which such evenings are sometimes arranged for the younger ones is through gatherings arranged at some club or other by a so-called "entrepreneur" who decides that on thus-and-such a date in thus-and-such a club there will be a party. By promising them free tickets, he then enlists students in the various schools to advertise the party among, or even sell tickets to, their schoolmates. Usually the kids are promised that there will be some famous rock or rap musician or disc jockey at the party.

With the exception of the kids themselves, it may not surprise anyone to learn that on the night in question the personage fails to show up. Still, if the entrepreneur has been successful in getting rid of his tickets, there is noise and smoke and crowding enough to feel like the approximation of a party.

If he has not been successful, the partygoers will be disappointed and full of complaint. The clubs in which such parties take place may not according to law serve any alcohol when the young ones take over, but many an impulse to complain about how the evening has worked out can, it seems, be quieted by the pot and ecstasy and LSD generously available in the club's bathrooms.

Without such arranged occasions, of course, kids can always find some kind of club in which to dance the night away in a reasonably innocent fashion while disregarding the antics in the lavatories. But the truth is, they are never far from the borders of innocence and safety. And the last couple of years have been witnessing an even newer style of youthful entertainment, called "the rave." A rave is a gathering of kids whose musical taste has moved beyond rap and heavy metal to advanced electronic music called "techno." ("What Stravinsky would be writing if he were alive today," said a deejay who specializes in raving to *Time* magazine.) It seems that this new kind of occasion, like the music on which it is based, was not so long ago a fairly exclusive taste. But like all youthful novelties it has inevitably found its way into the hands of Madison Avenue and the merchandisers.

Ecstasy, theoretically nonaddictive but potentially very dangerous, appears to be the drug of choice among the "ravers," who are generally recognizable by their wide-bottomed pants, strings of plastic beads, and—what seems to me of special interest—in the case of female ravers, plastic baby pacifiers worn around the neck.

Oh, how all alone those club-goers and ravers must feel by morning.

The second symptom of the frightening length of that parental thread has to do with sex. For by all accounts many of the girls seem to have found themselves quite bereft of the means to refuse or resist sexual involvement with the boys of their acquaintance, no matter how uninterested they might be. Neither the belligerence against males relied on by the earlier feminists nor the preoccupation with rape and AIDS of Katie Roiphe's contemporaries seems to have proven useful to these young ones as a technique for protecting themselves from doing what they do not wish to do.

So, and only so, could there have been invented the latest highly creative means girls have found to resist having sex with boys, namely, by practicing fellatio on them: "Unzip your fly and let's have done with it." Nor does this custom pertain only to established couples. Evidently it may be practiced between any two kids who happen to find themselves together under a variety of circumstances. Actually it's brilliant: the girls remain virgins, and the boys—the boys no doubt can't believe their luck.

Or can't they? There was a time, one or two generations back, when having a girl, as they used to say, "go down" on you would have seemed to a heterosexual teenage boy something he could only dream of. And that such a girl should also do so without exacting a price of any kind except perhaps that he be friendly and behave nicely would have seemed—nay, have been—beyond his wildest dreams. But for this once only dreamed-of experience to become merely everyday practice, might he not, say after a couple of years, become just a bit jaded, perhaps even find his sexual energies mysteriously flagging? There is an American tradition in song and story of the married man with an incorrigibly unresponsive wife whose sexual energies begin on that account to falter. True, a boy can almost always be counted on to be a human being with sexual energy to burn. Still, can he really over the course of some

time encounter girl after girl who is willing to service him
while remaining uninvolved and without beginning to feel just
a little bit alienated? After all, if it is simply release of pressure
he is after, a boy can easily service himself.

For what can this new sexual convention mean under the aspect of that currently most neglected of all eternal conditions,
namely, a boy's inborn desire for conquest? He cannot be a sexual hero because nowadays girls call all the shots: they either
casually minister to him or, if they happen to feel like it, charge
him with rape. Nor can he test his strength by acting as the
protector of women and girls, for it has been decreed that such
a "role" is sexist. Even joining the Marines won't do it anymore because nowadays in the Marine Corps there will be girls
right beside him trying to prove that they are as tough as he.
Later when he marries, any of his conquests in the world of
work will count for little, because according to the now-
established social ethos his wife either will also be a conqueror
or will have been socialized to belittle the "mere" fact that he
supports his family in better than minimal style.

Thus in a bitter irony of his young life, those girls who are
willing to service him at the drop of his pants while contriving
to remain "pure" themselves turn out, no doubt all unconsciously, to be acting out what is underneath it all merely
another version of feminism's brutal attitude toward him.
Suppose, for instance, that the woman whose story from a
Women's Lib anthology I have cited in an earlier chapter—the
one who after a hard day at work followed by having to clean
up the dinner dishes is sexually approached by her husband—
had merely wiped her hands and sighed, "Okay, drop your
pants and let's get on with it." Chances are that after a while he
would not have summoned the energy to approach her again
in that particular way very often, if at all.

In other words, it took another generation of really jaded, knowing, and needy girls to solve her problem.

When the sixties and seventies "kids" came back indoors from their demonstrations and those who did not make their way into law school or medical school discovered the possibilities of Wall Street or the computer chip, they were setting the stage for handing on to the next generation what may be the most all-around privileged life ever seen in an aristocracy-less society. And it seems that, as in the case of the aristocracy, some of the children were greatly benefited by their special advantage while at the same time many others appeared to be on their way to ruin because of it. In the first group are those most mysterious of all children, the ones who are self-sufficient and whose advantages are made full use of right from the start. These are as rare as they are mysterious, their most accomplished exemplar in twentieth-century history being Winston Churchill. In the second group are those whose cries for help in learning to accept themselves go unanswered. For where there is no real pinch of need, pride can sometimes be hard to come by, whereas self-hatred takes no one alive any effort at all, lurking as it does inside for each of us, waiting to pounce.

In any case, one very common substitute for genuine pride is the appearance of defiance. There have always been some people who have lived by gestures of defiance: bohemian women took many lovers; radical sixties boys refused to shave or cut their hair; and how many of us began to smoke in early adolescence precisely because we were told how bad it was for us?

But the recent style of defiant gesturing among the young is not intended to announce their wish to disturb conventional society, for truth to tell, as long as they don't kill anyone, nowadays that society could hardly care less about what its children do—until, that is, they cook up some unignorable crisis. No, the defiance that is being expressed by the young nowadays seems to be directed primarily against themselves, against such things about themselves as the good looks of their youth and their capacity to feel pain. For many among them have taken to having themselves tattooed all over like so many drunken sailors, and what is more distressing, they also find it in some way pleasing to stick rings and pins into virtually every part of their body—noses, brows, lips, tongues, navels, and one hesitates to imagine where else.

Years ago I watched on cable a televised convention of the pornography industry that was taking place in New York, and there was a woman, a famous and highly successful porn star, who was proudly displaying the fact that she had a large safety pin from which hung a little bell pinned through her labia. What she thought this was about it would have been hard to say, but surely it could have had nothing to do with the desire to stir anyone's lust, and in addition to her wishing to shock might very easily have had something to do with self-loathing, acknowledged or unacknowledged. Whenever I see a girl with a pierced lip, I cannot help thinking of that porn star, for whatever else it is, a beringed or bestudded lip is surely not for kissing.

Nor does it seem likely that many of them can be conscious of the original source of this new fashion of theirs: that what they are doing with their tattoos and piercings is in fact decking themselves out to look like what the homosexuals call "rough trade"—the truck drivers to whom so-called "gay" men go in the hope of being beaten and humiliated. For many of the young people so accoutered are after all not that much more than children, and not nearly as knowing as they imagine themselves to be. Why then, in the name of God, are they doing this to themselves?

This question has been given a couple of quite unsatisfying answers by certain experts on adolescent behavior. The kids are merely following the fashion, no matter how much it hurts, is one answer. But after all, other self-inflictions of pain for the sake of fashion, such as the ladies of the nineteenth century who strapped themselves into corsets intended to give them eighteen-inch waists, did so in order to conform to the going ideas of beauty, not to make themselves shocking or ugly. Another expert explanation is that all this is a rebellion against having to be "nice" children. This idea on the face of it seems to make more sense; rebellion is after all one of the standard explanations on offer nowadays for most forms of untoward behavior by the young. But, I cannot help asking, if that is the case, why are they taking it out on *themselves* so heavily? Why not steal a couple of hundred dollars from the old folks' wallets, or rob a candy store, instead? That would surely get both their parents' and the community's attention to their refusal to be nice—indeed, from the look of things it would do so a good deal more quickly and would involve a whole lot less pain.

No, it seems to me that it is clearly they themselves, and neither the wish to be stylish among their peers nor the desire to upset their parents, who are the real objects of this self-mutilation. When I was young I knew a girl who used to pull out her hair. It was a nervous tic; first she pulled out all her eyebrows and after that she went to work on her head, getting ever closer to the point of making herself bald. We all believed we understood her: she had a kid sister who was the most beautiful girl in town—like a pot of honey to the bees was this sister to the boys—so what she was doing, we said, was trying to attract attention to herself. "A cry for help," we all said, feeling very wise. We were close, but not quite up to recognizing what we were either too young, or just didn't wish, to know.

The truth was, she hated herself fiercely and was pulling out her hair not to get attention but to punish herself for her very existence. What she hated herself for might have had to do with her sister (who in the end, by the way, had a miserable time) but—who knows?—it might just as easily have had to do with something else, something then hidden from us. Though I had not given her a thought for something like fifty years, looking around me at all these pierced children, I nowadays find myself wondering from time to time how her life turned out.

Another thing that certain groups of boys, particularly those growing up in the most well-heeled suburbs, have taken to doing is adopting both the sartorial styles and demeanor of the inner-city black gang members. Their classmates call them "wiggers," which is intended to stand for "white niggers"—in some places they call one another "thugs"—and they offer some sad little swaggering imitation of those they take to be the really bad black brothers: beltless pants pulled down to mid-buttocks and thickly gathered around the ankles, monstrously expensive sneakers, heads shaved up to the crown or kept dirty and combed into Rastafarian-style dreadlocks. Aside from walking around in a hallucinogenic haze and using the word "mothahfuckah" at least twice in every sentence, it is not altogether clear just how really bad they are capable of being. This stunt strikes me as having some resemblance to the muddy and unhappy communes of yore to which these kids' counterparts in the 1960s fled in order to feel that they were escaping the ordinary solid bourgeois lives their families and society were holding out to them. Eventually they came back home, set back by a few years in taking up the lives that would once have been handed to them on a silver platter and occasionally feeling nostalgia (or at least pretending to) for their days in the mud.

That way they are able to have it all—a romantically remembered past and a solid and comfortable present.

The "wiggers" also seem to me to be expressing the need to do something at least make-believe brave in their suburban world of endless ease and goodies. It is as if they are saying to the self-satisfied enlightened souls who dominate the world around them, "You love black folks so much even though there is hardly a one to be seen around these parts? Here, we'll provide you with some, and see how you like it!" This bears a certain resemblance to my old argument with the fine liberal people in my hometown, only writ large and ugly, for there is something deeply ugly about the sight of privileged kids making a romantic pretense of being people whose lives, if they are not literally led in and out of prison, are in any case a futureless hell. "For the rich to play at being poor," says a character in Lillian Hellman's play *Toys in the Attic*, "is a dirty game." Maybe it is the dirtiest of all.

But it would be easy for those who adopt the pose to stop being "wiggers," or if not easy, at least possible to do without some major inner eruption. All it would take is to feel even the faintest stirrings of consideration for the long, long life ahead, perhaps even just the faintest glimmer of ambition at the prospect of going far away from home to some college that will be forgiving of their wasted teenage years. Or maybe it would take just one weekend spent on the streets of some dangerous neighborhood, trying to get away with doing their imitation black swagger. Their parents may be biting their tongues and trying to appear sympathetic with their children's "wiggerly" behavior, but almost certainly it would not be greeted with any brotherly gestures of fellow feeling by those denizens of the ghetto toward whom they aspire.

No doubt the rings and pins and the tattoos could also be

stashed, or burned, away some day in the not too distant future. But the self-hatred they bespeak cannot be shut off quite so easily. For it is not, and in the nature of things cannot be, a merely individual matter to be dealt with through some kind of psychotherapy: there are simply too many of them, young men and women and kids, all doing the same kinds of things to themselves. Nor can this spate of self-mutilation in turn be unrelated to the veritable plague of anorexia that has been spreading rapidly among America's young girls and women.

Self-starvation used to be a rather rare condition, usually requiring at least some amount of hospitalization. Now, in a no doubt somewhat milder form, it is so widespread as to boggle the mind. Again, many social theorists would tell us that for many girls anorexia is at bottom a means for staying in style, since fashion has for years now been dictating that women be exaggeratedly skinny. This is not an unpersuasive point. During the years that the clothes designers, who were for a considerable time almost exclusively homosexual, were attempting to keep women looking like boys, anyone with large breasts was hard put to find anything attractive to wear. Such an explanation for an eating disorder might seem to be more applicable to bulimia, something confessed to by many a model and movie star whose appetite was healthy but whose professional need to be very thin set them off on a steady round of eat-and-vomit. But even so, bulimia, like anorexia, must often be a more complicated case of self-denial than something dictated, say, by the demands of the beauty profession. For I know of certain perfectly ordinary-seeming young married women whose routine of wolfing down food and then giving it back they have managed, feeling shamed by it, to keep secret from their husbands for years. There must be many cases in which the impulses behind the bulimic refusal to keep the nourishment one offers oneself and the anorexic refusal to accept nourishment in the first place cannot be so far apart, though the latter seems clearly to be a far more dangerous condition.

But why is it only females, especially young ones, who are afflicted by this current spreading epidemic of eating disorders? The clothes designers, who appear to be relenting somewhat toward women with breasts and hips, have taken to doing a lot of advertising using the images of slender waif-like boys, and yet one almost never hears tell of a new generation of bulimic or anorexic young boys. Perhaps the answer can be found in what we know about the women who were kept alive as laborers in the Nazi murder camps and whose lack of needed nourishment led to the cessation of menstruation. Perhaps, that is, anorexia is the affliction of young girls who wish to stave off the arrival of menstruation, and with it, of womanhood and ultimately motherhood. The need to starve their bodies, then, would be an expression of their loathing for what nature has decreed that their bodies are to become and the various womanly roles it has decreed that they are to play.

But how, in that case, could one fail to associate the terrible spread of something that was not that long ago a relatively rare pathology with the rebellion against womanhood itself so angrily declared by the founders of the movement for Women's Liberation? For in the end the liberation originally sought by this movement, now somewhat moderated but still reverberant, was liberation from the ultimately inescapable nature of womanhood itself.

As I write these words, I know that they are going to occasion more than one angry outcry. I have grown accustomed over the years to being greeted with anger whenever I have suggested some connection between the movement's philosophy and certain of the unhappy consequences that have

followed from it—or merely pointed out the logical implications of some Women's Lib argument. And now that I have
drawn a connection between the movement and the positively
self-destructive self-hatred of young girls, no doubt another
storm will be a-brewing. So be it. All people involved in radical movements seem to hate the idea that what they are saying
may have implications that differ significantly from their de-
claratory meaning. In the case of the women's movement, one
of its chief and most influential philosophers, Betty Friedan,
seems to think that the bill of indictment brought by her movement against society's cruel and unjust treatment of women
down through the ages has not the slightest bearing on its attitude to men. "Hostile to men?" she has said, as if she had just
invented an arithmetic in which two plus two equals three.
"Why, we have never been hostile to men!" And—lo and behold!—there came the birth of sexual-harassment law, under
which hundreds of millions of dollars have been paid by employers to women who claimed that they were too weak and
delicate to ensure that some man would bother them no more,
by, for example, slamming their knees against the gentleman's
groin—a tried-and-true method that any female factory
worker could have taught them. And for their younger sisters
there was the invention of date rape, a happy expedient for the
young lady who for one reason or another regrets her having
neglected to hold off.

The shock and outrage of Mrs. Friedan's *semblables et soeurs*
would no doubt be doubled should it be suggested that her
movement has been responsible for more than one seriously
unkind thought about children. Forget about the horrible
things said about the very young by the likes of such feminist
heroines as Gloria Steinem and Germaine Greer—not to mention the mother of them all, Simone de Beauvoir. With or

without open intent, by its view of what a woman's life should properly look like the movement is implicitly antimotherhood. Why else would it have taken so many years for women intent on storming the citadel of career to discover in themselves an unfulfilled longing to have a child? And why, following the birth of a just-under-the-biological-wire baby, should a woman on the way to professional success be startled to discover in herself a deep reluctance to leave this baby in the care of others? Something had clearly been missing from the women's-movement assumptions about what such a woman's life ought ideally to be.

The feminists had for some time been asking for government-funded day care—this was part of their general diet of demand—and lately they have grown more and more vociferous about the need for government-subsidized day-care centers (what else would constitute the famous "village" of Hillary Rodham Clinton's dreams?). Moreover, they have found backing from a few allegedly distinguished psychologists, who have produced studies to show that babies in day care thrive better than they do at home with their mothers.

Can anyone but an unthinking, or resentful, ideologue (or a social scientist in the ideological swim) even pretend to believe that?

How, then, is one to resist the idea that one way or another all those self-mutilating or self-starving girls who have appeared in such frightening numbers all around us are the products of a culture seized by a decades-long bout of female self-hatred?

⤚12⤙

Where the Boys Are

BUT ASIDE FROM FEELING sorry for those little girls, most of whom have yet to leave their teens, it is the boys with whom they hang out who are in some ways even more to be worried about. For, as the social philosopher George Gilder warned us as long ago as the early seventies in his books *Sexual Suicide* and *Naked Nomads,* the true health and welfare of a man depends on some woman's insistence that he harness his energies for the defense and support of her and the family they will make together. For making this simple observation, Gilder was nearly drawn and quartered by the deaconesses of the high church of Women's Liberation, for women were at that point declaring their freedom from being dependent on men for anything at all.

Alas, Gilder's warning has been proven right. Not all that long after it was first issued, young women began to run into the phenomenon of the men who "wouldn't," or as they were likely to put it, "couldn't," make any kind of real commitment "just now." They were—and, alas, are still—the kind of young or by now not-so-young men whom a young woman could sleep with, even live with for a year or two, but who, should the subject ever come up, would whiningly profess themselves unable to "commit." And sooner or later the subject always did come up, because Women's Lib or no Women's Lib, sooner or later (nowadays, it seems later than sooner) young women are bound to discover in themselves an ever more pressing wish to be married. That just happens to be the way young women— or at least most of them—are.

So while long-married libbers began to gather in consciousness-raising groups whose basic purpose was for them to grouse about their husbands, younger women would also be getting together, to shake their heads (and perhaps their fists) at the seemingly endless number of young men their age who claimed to be "unready" to commit themselves. The secret was that under the influence of feminism, young women had been deprived of an opportunity to learn the age-old secret of how to ask them properly.

Let me explain. Now and then I used to have lunch with a young woman of my acquaintance who had a fairly successful beginning career as a journalist. We talked mostly about her ca- reer, the young of the seventies not being notable for the ability to stay for too long off the subject of themselves, but one day she began to talk about her feelings about marriage. Mostly these feelings had to do with what she would not put up with in married life. If, for instance, someone had the idea that she would spend her time scrubbing the kitchen floor, he would have another think coming, and so on in that vein, listing the various demands she would never let a husband make of her.

Finally I interrupted her and said, "You're a nice girl, and I like you. But tell me something: what would be in it for *him?*" So startled was she by this question that she turned uncharacteristically mute. Yet there is nothing earth-shattering about what I asked her; it just happens to be the question that underlies and informs every marriage.

For under normal modern circumstances, getting married has always been the result of a woman's persuading a man that if he will agree to husband her and father her children, she will in return make his having done so well worth his while. These thoughts are obviously never put into words in quite this way. And naturally, in the days before the sexual revolution sex would have been among the most obvious things she had to offer him. But even today, when sex is plentiful and easily come by—or so they tell us; some of us may still harbor the doubt that easy sex is quite as emotionally cost-free as the experts and journalists keep insisting—a man has other needs that only a wife can take care of.

That I should even feel impelled to mention what these needs are is a tribute to how far we have strayed from ordinary common sense about ourselves. But let's just begin with the need for a place of comfort and refuge from all the possible blows to his amour propre that a man can be made to suffer out there in the world of getting and spending. Then there is his need to have a place where he can count on some affection and respect—and maybe even some truly intimate friendship. Home, it used to be said, is the place where you can scratch wherever it itches.

Women, too, need affection and friendship, and to be able to scratch whatever itches. But women are different: more capable of creating a place of refuge for themselves, and in general more capable of looking after the small things that are really the big things. What they need of men most of all is a place of shelter and protection for their children. As any woman who has had to support herself for any length of time can tell you, this is no small matter.

In short, marriage is a deal, an exchange of promissory notes made out in separate currencies. The women who have in recent years demanded of their husbands that they be indistinguishable from themselves in the household—that they cook, clean, and look after the children in maternal fashion—to the extent that they succeed may one day wake up in a state of unnameable discontent. One of the currently popular forms taken by the demand that men become more feminine is the insistence that they learn to show their feelings as women do, preferably including the easy shedding of tears. But to ask men to behave like women is not a loving demand; over time, it becomes more like a stealthy move in a game of Gotcha.

Indeed, when I see couples living under the new dispensations of feminism I often wonder what would happen to them if they suddenly became poor and needed to shoulder their respective responsibilities without the luxury of being able to play around with the natural order of things. For after all—though this observation, too, may be greeted with howls of outrage—what Women's Lib calls "feminism" is a game that is played in comfort only by the members of the upper middle class.

Which brings me to my anxieties about my American grandsons and all the young boys of their present circumstance. For the society in which they live has become engaged in what can only be called a conspiracy against them. For example, in grammar school, should they fidget or misbehave after the universal fashion of little boys, they could in a trice find themselves being drugged with Ritalin (street name: speed)—with what effect on their later life no one really knows and no one in authority seems to care. That little boys cannot cease from wiggling around until they have been alive for quite a number of years is something any mother knows—and every teacher also once knew (which was why, at least when I was going to school way back in the Middle Ages, the class would have to stop every now and then and stand up and do a few exercises). Most little girls, on the other hand, can from a very early age not only sit still but sit still, if need be, with their hands folded. That is why they have generally done better in school, at least until adolescence sets in and unnerves them. And nowadays the teachers seem to have decided that they will not put up with any little-boy behavior, and have somehow found psychiatrists willing to help them by diagnosing the wiggling boys as suffering from the disease called attention-deficit disorder and calming them down with their daily dose of drugging.

In addition to their being regularly fed an amphetamine, as if being a boy were a kind of sickness, the textbooks they are most likely to be taught from will be shot through with tributes to the bravery and glorious achievements of women, blacks, and American Indians with little left over for an occasional pink-skinned male—an old-time president maybe. And later on, the novels and poems they will be assigned to read in their English classes will most likely be written by women—*The Color Purple* by Alice Walker, say, or *The Bell Jar* by Sylvia Plath, for example—which will no doubt be, and certainly should be, very soon forgotten, meanwhile, however, strengthening the message that boys' own passions, needs, longings, and sense of life count for nothing. And having been so meagerly educated, they will be required to sweat bullets about getting into some college, where they will most likely be meagerly educated once again.

But probably worst of all, for decent, well-brought-up boys,
is the way they have been left with almost no innocent means
for testing their manly valor. Take a very simple case. The last
thing an American boy is nowadays apt either to hear or to read
is that girls, being the weaker and more delicate sex, need to be
protected. Anyone who tried to tell them such a thing would,
of course, instantly be set upon by a gender posse. Thus many
of them grow up feeling not brave with girls but, on the contrary, some unexpressed combination of clumsy and resentful.
Even when they score sexually, they are these days often required to play the passive party.

Not so long ago, the country was riveted with horror at a
string of schoolyard killings, most famously the one in the
Denver suburb of Littleton. But Littleton was the last in a
series. Before that was West Paducah, Kentucky, where a
fourteen-year-old boy killed three fellow students and
wounded five; Pearl, Mississippi, where a young boy went after
seven of his classmates with considerable success and took out
his mother as well; and Jonesboro, Arkansas, where two boys,
eleven and thirteen, put on army fatigues, went to school, set
off a fire alarm, and picked off four children and a teacher as
they came outside for what they supposed was a fire drill. Naturally, all these incidents of killing schoolmates (and there were
a couple of others along the same lines) very quickly brought
out the usual experts. Members of the antigun lobby said all
this was the fault of guns and the people who kept them in
their houses. Members of the anti-TV lobby said these killings
were merely copycatting the steady, inescapable violence on
TV. And some child-psychiatric experts said these children
(boys only, please note) were lacking in the necessary amount
of contact with adults. And who can blame the experts, thin
and inadequate as their explanations seem? Such events posi-

tively cry out for someone to come along and give them a graspable explanation. But the guns were not made available to these boys; they stole them. Moreover, the endless violence on TV may be part of, but by itself would be hardly sufficient, an explanation. For long before television, it may be remembered, boys were drawn to games of imaginary violence, such as cops and robbers or cowboys and Indians, as well as simply given to pummeling one another in play for hours at a time.

No, the horrors of those schools and schoolyards were about something else, something unimaginable and at the same time not without reason. The two boys in Jonesboro explained to the authorities that they had hated their schoolmates, especially certain girls, for rejecting them. To my ear this, far more than anything said about these killings by the experts, has a special ring of truth. For I would like to meet the thirteen-year-old, boy *or* girl, who has not spent some weeks of his or her thirteen-year-old life feeling exactly the same way—that is, feeling rejected and unloved and hating someone or perhaps a whole group of someones as a result of this feeling.

But as I remember, there used to be various ways of expressing that emotion, spiteful and hurtful but considerably short of bloody murder: hate mail, threatening phone calls, spreading nasty rumors, writing dirty words on one's classmates' notebooks or chalking them on the sidewalks in front of their houses, getting into fist-fights, and slashing bicycle tires. But murder? And indiscriminate murder at that? The question, then, is not why so many of America's adolescents are easily made angry but why they no longer seem to find any genuinely adolescent outlets for their bouts of alienation, whether they be in relation to parents, to friends, or just to school itself.

I don't pretend to know any more than the experts do about why there should have been this sudden explosion of schoolboys killing their teachers and schoolmates. But I do know something about those boys, and others like them, and it isn't that they watch TV and don't have enough contact with adults (some in fact may have all too much). It's that the society in which they live, and in which we all live, will neither allow them on the one hand to grow up nor on the other hand to be real children at only the beginning of their journey to some genuine kind of adulthood. Consider, for instance, that few if any American boys have any truly responsible work to do or any serious way to know that they are pulling their weight in their families or communities—no wood to chop, no water to draw. And even if there were an opportunity to shoulder some genuine responsibility, the authorities wouldn't let them do it until that point in their teens by which usually a lot of indiscipline has already set in.

And American kids are infantilized in a lot of other ways as well, preeminent among them their almost never having to pay any genuine price for bad behavior, either at school, at home, or in the world at large.

But if the country's children are in some sense kept in an ersatz state of infancy from the lack of playing any serious role in the world, they are at the same time also deprived of their God-given entitlement to the comforting innocence of childhood. They are, for example, introduced to all the various issues concerning and surrounding sex way, way before they wish to be. To my mind there may be no greater sin against the psyches of children than the answering by adults of unasked questions about the fine points of sexual relations. This particular sin would be so easy and comforting to lay at the door of the media, but the truth is, it is being committed in the schools, in many of the books the authorities find it uplifting to include in their approved reading lists, to some extent even in their churches, and last but hardly least, in how the children's parents have been instructed by today's enlightened culture in how to "handle" the issue with them, that is, with full frankness, when the kids don't yet understand—and don't yet really want to understand—the half of it. Anyone who has ever been told a really dirty joke by a young child—as I, grandmother of seven boys, have been the audience to such a fair number of times—can see how very little of what they are talking about they actually comprehend. It is their innocence and not the joke that leaves one smiling.

But they are not to be allowed to keep that innocence for long. Their parents and schools would be made to feel remiss for leaving it to the children to determine when and what they are ready to learn about grown-up life—remiss and, oh horrors, even conservative. So there the children are: first knowing all about, and subsequently dabbling in, sex well beyond their years while at the same time deprived in every other area of their lives of the strength that comes from the feeling that their powers are in some palpable and measurable way useful to the world around them. In other words, they are neither children nor adults.

Where girls are concerned, this is evident to the naked eye, as (except in the case of school uniforms) they are permitted, perhaps even expected, to deck themselves out like so many prematurely grown women.[1] For boys, however, this situation of being neither one thing nor another is far, far more difficult than for girls, because most young females are already in some sense grown up at an early age. For whether they can articulate it or not, they more or less know what nature will one day call

---

1. While ironically, aging women can be seen all over the place trying to imitate the dress and demeanor of young girls.

on them to do. Watch a little girl with any passing baby and you will see something going on, some exchange, that can never take place between a baby and a little boy, no matter how kind and tender and affectionate he might be. The feminists who some years back set out to erase "gender differences" by imposing a strict reversal of their children's toys—dolls and tea sets for boys, trucks for girls, and so on—may have succeeded in creating some temporary confusion among their sons but can never have even come near to touching their daughters. Little boys are wide open in those early years, while little girls already know just what they're after. Later, to be sure, things usually reverse themselves. When the gonads acquire minds of their own, the boys with dolls are willy-nilly bound to be de-feminized by the onrush of hormones, if they have not been so already, while some of the girls may begin to struggle a little with the problem of who and what they are. For nowadays the members of the social world around them, and their mothers especially, press on them a variety of ambitions, and what they most deeply are, namely women-in-becoming, may get sub-merged—though usually not permanently. For a young woman may wish to be and do many things, but chances are wife and mother will figure prominently among them.

But as for boys, what is to become of them now that the cul-ture in which they live gives them no refuge or quarter? I don't mean professionally, to be sure: the world of seemingly endless innovation in which we find ourselves, though hardly any longer a place requiring exclusively masculine heavy lifting, is bound to continue to be in great need of them. But what is to become of their inner life if they continue to be subjected to a kind of continual low-grade fever of hostility toward what na-ture has decreed for them to be?

Take what may be the most egregious case of what I am

talking about, women in the military. The demand that women be integrated into every branch of the armed forces is a demand originally made by a group of women without a care in the world for either the armed power or the security of the United States. For them the army and navy and air force were just another sector of society into which they demanded the right of women to move on an equal footing. (Indeed, the truth is that if the country's military strength were to be considerably undermined, most of this particular group of activists would not shed a single tear.) The politicians surrendered, and the military was required to follow. What then happened was what anyone with a bit of ordinary horse sense might have predicted would happen. First, an easing up on the rigors of training,[2] and second, the rearing of the ugly head of s-e-x. This would then inevitably be followed by the leveling of charges of sexual harassment, and the wrecking of some distinguished military careers. What a great benefit to both women and society!

Some years ago I was in a party of people who were being shown around a naval base. First we visited a nuclear submarine, in which just to imagine spending weeks on a tour of duty was enough to give one an attack of claustrophobia. Whatever their motive for being what they are and doing what they do, those submariners are selfless heroes. Lately, and I suppose inevitably, there has been talk of allowing women to be submariners alongside the men. For someone in authority even to imagine the possibility of putting women into those tight quar-

---

2. The military spokesmen, of course, deny this vociferously, but common sense would tell anyone not totally blinkered by ideology that even the toughest women cannot withstand for long the rigors that used to be imposed on military trainees, or the kinds of punishment that would follow from someone's inability to meet the standard.

ters is an act of brutality toward the men that only a deeply hostile culture could have made possible.

After the sub, we visited the tender devoted to servicing it. For those who don't know about these things, the tender is a gigantic ship—a floating factory, actually—that meets up with the sub from time to time and provides (actually makes) whatever parts need replacing and whatever other services are required. Before the tour started, we were greeted by the tender's captain, who was to give us a brief orientation. Practically before he even introduced himself, the very first words out of his mouth, spoken as if he had been mechanically programmed, were, yes, there were women aboard the ship, and yes, they were both competent workers and first-rate seamen. Perhaps if he had waited even ten minutes before making this statement, it would not have been quite so clear just how much he resented the situation and the things he was being forced to say about it to the visiting public. According to an op-ed piece published in the *Wall Street Journal* (May 9, 2000) by Stephanie Gutmann, author of a vitally important book called *The Kinder, Gentler Military: Can It Fight?,* the captain's poorly concealed sentiment is widely shared among the officers and enlisted men, who "use words like 'sterile,' 'sanitized,' 'babyish,' 'corporate,' 'totalitarian,' and 'micromanaged' to describe it." She quotes another soldier who says, "It's like a politically correct fish bowl." In other words, just as they had not in their earlier years been allowed to be just children, thanks to the fact that women now share both their quarters and their training, they are not allowed to become red-blooded men under the ministrations of the army.

But even if women had not won the fight to be taken into the military arm in arm with the men, America's boys would nowadays be deprived of one very important boon to their spiritual formation: the idea that they might one day be called upon to defend their country and that there is no higher or braver or more manly a thing to do than that. Of course, society can't really fake a thing like that, and nothing makes it as believable as a genuine international crisis. But Richard Nixon did an incalculable disservice to the psychic life of American boys when, in order to buy a little social peace from the disaffected young of his time in the presidency, he helped to turn the military into a voluntary institution seeming to be dedicated mainly to the process of career training.[3] Think of the TV recruiting commercials that are the most frequently broadcast. "Be all that you can be" is the slogan. Not "Be a good man," "Be a brave man," "Be a strong man," "Attach yourself to something greater than you," or simply, "Be a man." (Think of the lawsuits *that* would engender these days.) Not even "Be better than you—and all the teachers and mean girls in the eighth grade—ever thought you could be."

No more in Cambridge, Massachusetts, or Park Avenue or Harlem or the South Side of Chicago or Watts does society nowadays provide a boy with any kind of genuine rite of passage into manhood. I mean by this something you have to go through because your society needs you to do it and requires you to do it. The two most important of these rites, it seems to me, are preparing yourself to defend your country, militarily and/or morally, and preparing yourself to court and marry a woman. And nowadays both have virtually been ruled out. The government will have little to do with it, and the women even less. Thus chances are that the boys who do make it into genuine manhood will have had to achieve it mostly on their

---

3. Bill Clinton did Nixon one better by turning it into an agency for doing social work in other people's crises.

own. Many, of course, do. But no thanks to the culture that surrounds them.

For the others, if they are growing up prosperous and well cosseted, money will help to provide a simulacrum of manliness. They can zip around in sporty automobiles, for instance, and engage in all sorts of grown-up leisure-time activities. They can roam the world over and savor all sorts of exotic experiences. They can, in other words, become sophisticated and knowing far beyond the capacity of less privileged men twice their age. And at the opposite economic end, that is, in the slums of the inner city, they, too, can enjoy a patina of manliness, in a certain kind of masculine swagger and lawlessness and violence. Moreover, beyond any likely achievement of their rich counterparts is the siring of many illegitimate babies, whom they for the most part either neglect or mistreat. But beyond their differences, there is one thing the two have in common: their lack of genuine investment in some future, whether future generations or, what is basically the same thing, the future of their society. It is not pleasant to imagine what these unmanned boys will look like when they are middle-aged.

Meanwhile, when it comes to my own grandsons, who are neither rich nor poor, and whose experiences with girls—which, whether successful or unsuccessful, I would rather not know too much about—I am just as bad as the next one in both indulging and excusing them. But if any of them should show up one day with some girl who was trying to get them in touch with their feminine side, my heart might just break.

⁓ Postscript ⁓

THE BIBLE SAYS that the span of man's life is three score years and ten. I have already passed a certain distance beyond that milestone and yet, except for an occasional twinge here and there and the discovery that I am no longer inclined to run either up or down a long flight of steps, most of the time I sinfully imagine that I am going to go on for a long, long time.

To begin with, I am curious to see by what complicated tricks of mind and psyche the women of the enlightened world will be working their way to some more comfortable sharing of this earth with all those men whose essential part in their lives they have so carelessly come to make light of. I also feel a great need to learn if all those self-mutilating and self-starving little girls and out-of-control boys ever find some genuine medicine for their disquiet.

And most important of all, there are those ten grandchildren, whose lives I most urgently desire to keep an eye on for a good while longer. Each of them is gripping in his and her own way, and each seems to me to occupy too interesting a place in the universe to be easily dispensed with. Besides, without knowing much more of their stories, how can I ever really know how my own comes out?

At fleeting moments, I even find myself greedily playing with the thought of great-grandchildren. My mother died before she met any of the twelve that would have been hers. My mother-in-law, on the other hand, who lived to be ninety-two, was lucky enough to know all fourteen of her great-grandchildren. But then she was so riddled with anxiety—living as she did in a world she no longer either approved of or permitted herself to understand—that truth to tell, she found little pleasure in them. For a while she pretended, and then finally even gave up the pretense.

But then in thinking this way about great-grandchildren, I am committing what to Judaism is among the heaviest of sins, namely, attempting to hasten the outcome. I should, and in fact do, have enough to be grateful for without hoping to imagine future pleasures (except, perhaps, that very final "pleasure" that my father, lying there in that hospital bed, once taught me to be mindful of).

I believe it to be true, as I have been trying to say in the preceding chapters, that in some ways life—including the thirties Depression, the war, and postwar struggles—used in many ways to be better than it is now. But at the same time I am conscious of how much of an old fogy that makes me sound. Would I, then, begrudge my fellow Americans, especially the young ones, any of the ease and advantages of the economic glories being heaped on us all by the American economy in all its flexibility and openness to the new? The answer is a

resounding no. Feeling pinched does not make people any nicer or morally better, something I hope that my own story fully illustrates.

Nor do I believe, as some current piety would have it, that old-fashioned small-town life, while almost by definition more neighborly, is at bottom any more tender and loving. Sometimes the brutality of people living very close together—as in those presently much celebrated extended families—can be positively crippling in its cruelties.

But living as we do in the ever-changing, positively kaleidoscopic world of new technologies, previously unseen prosperity, and new freedom, especially from a number of former barely tolerable miseries of the body, has willy-nilly sent us all flying into an uncharted territory of the mind and spirit where we find ourselves wandering around insufficiently protected by our respective traditions. That mixture of groups of believing Christians and Jews known to the journalists simply as "the Religious Right" have responded to all this by attempting to isolate themselves from both the bewilderments and the temptations of this new world. So far they have been more or less successful, but what, in the long run, of their offspring? In a cyber-world, isolation does not seem to me to be a safe answer. Nor does railing against the sins of the media, as if those were sins into which the press and movie industry and television studios had originally fallen and into which they were now attempting to drag the rest of us. For in the long run the media get around to selling us what we buy; that is the business they are in.

I cannot claim to know how we are to find our way out of this: how the old, for instance, can learn to be truly grateful for the extra life being granted them; or the young discover the riches of a truly responsible life; or the women return to loving

themselves for their genuine strengths, and the men, for theirs. But after all these many years of taking part and observing, I am certain that part of our deep discomfort in this most comfortable of all possible worlds has to do with our having fallen into a potentially very dangerous combination of arrogance and deep bewilderment. Perhaps if this society as a whole spent some part of its time in a state of simple gratitude for the beneficence bestowed upon it; and perhaps if we individuals were daily to remind ourselves that this beneficence is a gift, not a mere entitlement, we might at last assume the posture necessary for finding our way out of all the treacherous byways of this new territory and back to where our nature truly beckons us—and lead our bewildered children behind us.